How to Use
1-2-3

How to Use
1-2-3

CHRISTOPHER J. BENZ

Illustrated by
SARAH ISHIDA AND DAVE FEASEY

Ziff-Davis Press
Emeryville, California

Copy Editor	Kelly Green
Technical Reviewer	Heidi Steele
Project Coordinator	Ami Knox
Proofreader	Ami Knox
Cover Illustration	Regan Honda
Cover Design	Regan Honda
Book Design	Dennis Gallagher/Visual Strategies, San Francisco
Screen Graphics Editor	P. Diamond
Technical Illustration	Sarah Ishida, Dave Feasey, and Cherie Plumlee
Word Processing	Howard Blechman
Page Layout	M.D. Barrera
Indexer	Kayla Sussell

Ziff-Davis Press books are produced on a Macintosh computer system with the following applications: FrameMaker®, Microsoft® Word, QuarkXPress®, Adobe Illustrator®, Adobe Photoshop®, Adobe Streamline™, MacLink® *Plus*, Aldus® FreeHand™, Collage Plus™.

If you have comments or questions or would like to receive a free catalog, call or write:
Ziff-Davis Press
5903 Christie Avenue
Emeryville, CA 94608
1-800-688-0448

ISBN 1-56276-316-4

Manufactured in the United States of America
⊛ This book is printed on paper that contains 50% total recycled fiber of which 20% is de-inked postconsumer fiber.
10 9 8 7 6 5 4 3 2 1

TABLE OF CONTENTS

ACKNOWLEDGMENTS

 I owe the sheer beauty of this book to the combined graphical wizardry of illustrator Sarah Ishida, layout artist M.D. Barrera, and screen-shot expert P. Diamond.

Despite its highly graphical appeal, a learning guide such as this still depends on solid ideas and understandable language. Acquisitions editor Eric Stone deserves my greatest thanks for providing me a robust base for this book—and for giving the task of writing it! Thanks also to copy editor Kelly Green for keeping my words in line; to technical editor Heidi Steele for making sure I was telling the truth; and to project coordinator Ami Knox for making sure everything got done on time and in the correct order, and for checking up on the rest of us.

Many other professionals were critical parts of the publishing process. At Ziff-Davis Press, these people were Howard Blechman, Bruce Lundquist, Tony Jonick, Margo Hill, Cheryl Holzaepfel, Cindy Hudson, and everyone in the Accounting Department. At Lotus Development Corporation, it was Cheryl Fields.

Finally, my most personal thanks go to Dad, even if he *does* occasionally ask me when I'm going to get a *real* job.

INTRODUCTION

You're a beginning user of Lotus 1-2-3 Release 5 for Windows. Maybe your math is a little rusty. Maybe you're not even sure what a spreadsheet program is. You're not looking to produce a work of art. You don't need hotshot shortcuts. You just need to get this thing to work.

How to Use 1-2-3 is for you. In this concise, colorful book, you'll see 1-2-3 work right before your eyes, step by step, task by task. When done reading, you'll be a comfortable, confident user of the most important features 1-2-3 offers. Entering data, performing calculations, creating charts—these and many other indispensable skills will be right at your fingertips.

Each chapter of this book presents up to five related topics. Because each topic spans two facing pages, everything you need to know about a topic is in front of you at one time. Just follow the numbered steps around the pages, reading the text and looking at the pictures. It's really as easy as it looks!

Colorful, realistic examples are included to help you understand how you might use each feature of 1-2-3. You may wish to enter and work with the sample data as you learn, but doing so is not at all mandatory. If you want to stay focused on your own work and use this book as a reference, you'll find it well suited for that purpose.

Even experienced computer users occasionally stumble into unfamiliar territory. Read the "Tip Sheet" accompanying each topic to learn more about the occasional pitfall or quirky feature—or just how to make the most of 1-2-3.

You'll find special sections called *Try It* at strategic spots in this book. A Try It section is a hands-on exercise that gives you valuable practice with the skills you've acquired to that point. As you read a Try It section, be sure to follow each step at your computer.

To get the most out of this book, read it in sequence. If you have any prior experience with Microsoft Windows, Lotus 1-2-3, or electronic spreadsheets in general, you may be familiar with the information in the first two chapters. Skimming those chapters, however, will provide a useful refresher of important concepts and terms.

I'm eager to know your reactions to this book. Please mail any comments and suggestions for future editions to:

Christopher J. Benz
c/o Ziff-Davis Press
5903 Christie Avenue
Emeryville, CA 94608
Internet: 6229438@mcimail.com

Enjoy!

CHAPTER 1

What Is Electronic Accounting?

Electronic accounting is the management of financial data on a computer. Before the computer age, accounting was handled on unwieldy paper ledgers. These ponderous documents were understood by few people other than finance experts. Finding information was a challenge. Correcting data and making projections were major undertakings.

With electronic accounting, virtually anyone can understand and manage financial data. It takes just a few commands to find data buried anywhere in the company books. Projections and "what if" analyses take mere moments—and the computer performs all the calculations.

Your personal computer wasn't built with the ability to perform electronic accounting—or to do much of anything else. Just as a CD player needs CDs to make music, a computer needs *programs* to tell it what to do. A program that enables you to perform electronic accounting on your computer is called a *spreadsheet program,* and the data it manages is called a *spreadsheet.* Your computer probably also runs other programs such as word processors, databases, and games.

This book teaches you how to use one spreadsheet program: 1-2-3 Release 5 for Windows from Lotus Development Corporation of Cambridge, Massachusetts. 1-2-3 for Windows, often called simply "1-2-3," is widely regarded as one of the best spreadsheet programs around. Read on to find out why.

What Can a Spreadsheet Program Do?

Electronic spreadsheets vary in their capabilities, but almost all of them can help you manage and present data like that shown here. This relatively simple spreadsheet highlights many of the once-difficult things that spreadsheet programs now do routinely. Let's take a closer look.

 1 Most fundamentally, a spreadsheet program gives you an on-screen grid to work within. Each box in the grid (the intersection of a row and a column) is called a *cell*. Most of the time you will put numbers in cells, but sometimes you will enter text, such as column and row headings.

6 Finding data is a cinch. Tell your spreadsheet program you want the name of every department that spent more than $5,000 last quarter, and it will pluck this information without batting an eye.

2nd Qtr Totals > $5,000	
Dept.	**Total**
R & D	$7,999
Sales	$12,853

5 A modern spreadsheet program can instantly express your data as a chart. You need know very little about charting to take advantage of this capability.

 TIP SHEET

▶ It's worthwhile to know what spreadsheet programs do, but no doubt you're more eager to learn what *1-2-3* does—and how to do it. Relax. The rest of this book covers just that.

▶ Perhaps you're familiar with another spreadsheet program and are now switching to 1-2-3. Modern-day spreadsheet programs can all do pretty much the same things. The difference lies in how easy each task is, and you'll find that 1-2-3 is, overall, one of the easiest spreadsheet programs to use.

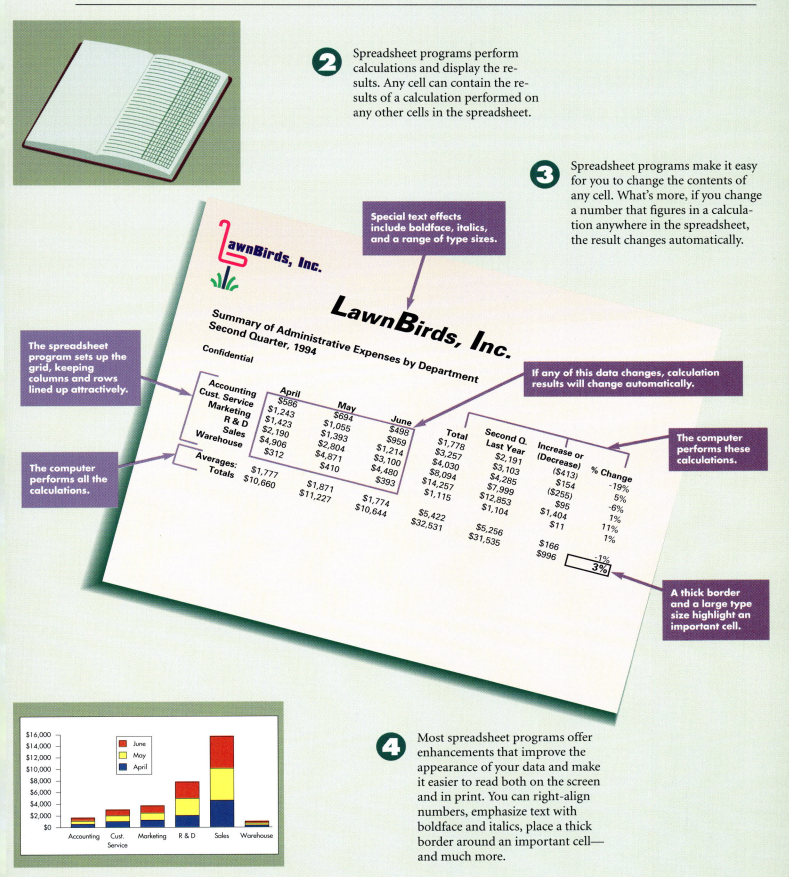

2 Spreadsheet programs perform calculations and display the results. Any cell can contain the results of a calculation performed on any other cells in the spreadsheet.

3 Spreadsheet programs make it easy for you to change the contents of any cell. What's more, if you change a number that figures in a calculation anywhere in the spreadsheet, the result changes automatically.

Special text effects include boldface, italics, and a range of type sizes.

The spreadsheet program sets up the grid, keeping columns and rows lined up attractively.

The computer performs all the calculations.

If any of this data changes, calculation results will change automatically.

The computer performs these calculations.

A thick border and a large type size highlight an important cell.

LawnBirds, Inc.

LawnBirds, Inc.

Summary of Administrative Expenses by Department
Second Quarter, 1994

Confidential

	April	May	June	Total	Second Q. Last Year	Increase or (Decrease)	% Change
Accounting	$586	$694	$498	$1,778	$2,191	($413)	-19%
Cust. Service	$1,243	$1,055	$959	$3,257	$3,103	$154	5%
Marketing	$1,423	$1,393	$1,214	$4,030	$4,285	($255)	-6%
R & D	$2,190	$2,804	$3,100	$8,094	$7,999	$95	1%
Sales	$4,906	$4,871	$4,480	$14,257	$12,853	$1,404	11%
Warehouse	$312	$410	$393	$1,115	$1,104	$11	1%
Averages:	$1,777	$1,871	$1,774	$5,422	$5,256	$166	-1%
Totals	$10,660	$11,227	$10,644	$32,531	$31,535	$996	**3%**

4 Most spreadsheet programs offer enhancements that improve the appearance of your data and make it easier to read both on the screen and in print. You can right-align numbers, emphasize text with boldface and italics, place a thick border around an important cell—and much more.

1-2-3 Is Your Spreadsheet Program

1-2-3 is a product—a brand, if you will. Just as there are different soft drinks on the market, many quite similar, so there are various spreadsheet programs, many excellent but none plainly superior. However, 1-2-3 has gained popularity among both beginning and experienced users because of its comfortable "look and feel" and its convenient, versatile features, many of which you'll master as you read this book. You may have heard of other spreadsheet programs such as Excel and Quattro Pro. These products compete with 1-2-3 for the hearts and dollars of people who perform electronic accounting.

▶ **①** 1-2-3 is not built into your computer. You buy 1-2-3 and install it on your computer much as you buy a CD and insert it in your CD player to play it. It might *seem* like 1-2-3 was built into your computer if someone else installed it on the computer's hard disk for you, or if you use a copy that's installed on your office network.

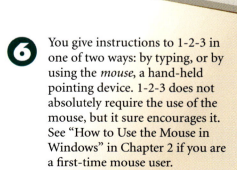

TIP SHEET

▶ **This book is about Release 5 of Lotus 1-2-3 for Windows. Unless you have Release 5, you cannot be sure that everything you read in this book applies to you. Check your 1-2-3 packaging to verify the release number if you're not sure of it.**

▶ **Chapter 2 of this book is for first-time computer users or first-time Windows users. If you can start Microsoft Windows, use the mouse, select commands from a menu, and make selections in a dialog box, skip ahead to Chapter 3. If you can't do all these things (or if you don't even know what they mean!), you'd best not skip ahead.**

⑥ You give instructions to 1-2-3 in one of two ways: by typing, or by using the *mouse*, a hand-held pointing device. 1-2-3 does not absolutely require the use of the mouse, but it sure encourages it. See "How to Use the Mouse in Windows" in Chapter 2 if you are a first-time mouse user.

2 1-2-3 is based on Microsoft Windows, a program that helps you manage the computing environment and run other programs. This means that 1-2-3's *interface* (the way you give commands to it and receive information from it) is similar to that of many other programs, including some you may already know how to use.

3 1-2-3 is quite well regarded. Many spreadsheet experts—and ordinary users, too—consider it the finest Windows-based spreadsheet program. You'll be using a program that has withstood the test of time and earned the respect of the computing community.

4 What makes 1-2-3 such a standout? Well, it has lots of useful features and plenty of convenient shortcuts for expert users. But most users, especially beginners, would answer in less tangible terms: "It's easy," or, "It feels right."

5 1-2-3 is a spreadsheet program, and it sports the same basic features as other modern spreadsheet programs. Like the other programs, it helps you manage, analyze, and present financial data.

CHAPTER 2

What Are DOS and Windows?

 DOS and Windows are programs that enable you to run all the programs you really *want* to run: your spreadsheet program (1-2-3), your word processor, your games, and so on.

DOS, short for *disk operating system,* moves information to and from the disks in your computer. Without an operating system, your computer cannot do anything useful for you. You cannot run a program such as 1-2-3 unless you tell DOS to copy it temporarily from a disk into *random-access memory* (RAM), a storage area that your computer can interact with quickly and directly. Likewise, you cannot electronically store and later reuse your data unless you have DOS copy it from RAM onto a disk.

Windows can simplify your role in directing these and many other affairs on your computer. It also provides a consistent and fairly appealing backdrop for Windows-based programs such as 1-2-3. Windows-based programs look comfortingly similar on the screen, and there are many similarities in the ways you work with them. If you've used any Windows-based program, certain 1-2-3 operations will be familiar to you.

You don't need to start DOS. It is running whenever you are using your computer. Windows, on the other hand, is an add-on program that you have the option of running as you use your computer. But Windows *must* be running before you can start 1-2-3 or any other Windows-based program. This chapter helps you start and run Windows. If you already know how to start Windows and use any Windows-based program, you can safely skip this chapter.

How to Start Windows from DOS

The heart and soul of DOS, at least from the user's viewpoint, is the *DOS prompt*. This is where DOS asks you for information and you provide it. By typing *commands* at the DOS prompt, you can run programs, check the contents of your disks, reset the time on your computer's internal clock, and much more. For now, the only DOS command you absolutely must know is the one to start Windows.

TIP SHEET

▶ Your computer may be set up to bypass the DOS prompt and start Windows automatically. If Windows has started, you'll see the words *Program Manager* somewhere on the screen. In this case, you can skip steps 4 and 5—whose purpose is, after all, to help you start Windows.

▶ Upon startup, some computers automatically run the *DOS Shell,* an interface designed to make DOS operations easier. If your computer is running the DOS Shell, you'll see the words *MS-DOS Shell* across the top of the screen. Hold down the Alt key as you type fx to exit the DOS Shell and face the DOS prompt. Then proceed with step 4.

▶ A consultant or office computer specialist may have set up a *custom menu* that appears in place of the DOS prompt. This menu should contain an entry for *Windows* (or possibly *Microsoft Windows* or *Windows 3.1* or a similar variation). To start Windows, you probably have to press the ↓ key until the Windows entry is highlighted, and then press Enter. However, you may have to consult with your consultant or office computer specialist to learn how the custom menu works.

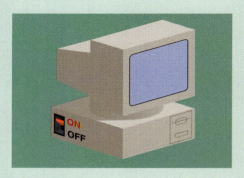

▶ **1** Switch on your computer and give it a minute or so to go through its wake-up ritual. When the computer is ready to accept information from you, it will ask you for the information or display the DOS prompt.

5 If the preceding step produced a message such as *Bad command or file name,* try typing **c:\windows\win** and pressing Enter. If that fails, try **d:\windows\win**. Still can't start Windows? Well, the possible reasons and solutions are too many to enumerate here, but a computer-savvy colleague should be able to help you in short order. Or call Microsoft technical support, which fields questions like yours routinely.

2 Provide any information the computer asks for, and press the Enter key when done. Some computers ask for the date and time. If your computer is on a *network*—a setup where personal computers in an office are hooked together to share information—it may ask you for your name and password. (Your office's network administrator can help you with this step.)

3 After providing any initial information your computer needs, you should see the DOS prompt. This is the way DOS asks you to give it a command. The most common DOS prompt looks like *C:\>* but it can vary considerably. You can easily start Windows no matter how the DOS prompt looks.

4 Type **win** and press the Enter key. On most computers, this command will start Windows. After a few seconds, you'll see the words *Program Manager* somewhere on the screen, indicating that Windows is now running. Skip the next step if this step worked fine.

How to Start a Program from Program Manager

Program Manager is a Windows-based program that comes with Windows. Its role is to make it easy to start *other* programs, including 1-2-3. Program Manager is your home base; it opens when you start Windows and remains open as long as Windows is running. This page shows how Program Manager might look when you start Windows. Then again, Windows is highly customizable, so your starting screen can look quite different.

1 A window is simply an on-screen box containing information. Like most Windows-based programs, Program Manager has an application window and lets you open multiple document windows inside it. In this screen there are six windows wholly or partially visible, as represented by six title bars.

Menu bar

Application window

Document window

Double-click to start the Paintbrush program.

6 Then, to start a program, locate its program item in a program group window, roll the mouse to point to the program name or icon, and double-click.

5 When you want to start a program, first open the program group window containing its program item. To open a program group window, roll the mouse on a flat surface until the arrow points to the group name or icon, and then click the left mouse button twice in rapid succession ("double-click").

2 An application window contains a program's *menu bar,* from which you issue commands. The application window for Program Manager also contains icons representing *program groups,* collections of related programs that you can run. The *title bar* of the application window contains the program name—in this case, Program Manager.

This user has seven program groups.

Active document window

3 There can be zero, one, or multiple document windows open at one time, but only one document window is *active.* The active document window is the one that will be affected by commands you issue. The title bar of each document window contains the document name, and the title bar of the active document window is highlighted.

Control Menu boxes

Title bars

Maximize and Minimize buttons

Program items. Double-click on any item to start the program.

Program groups. Double-click on any group to see its contents in a program group window.

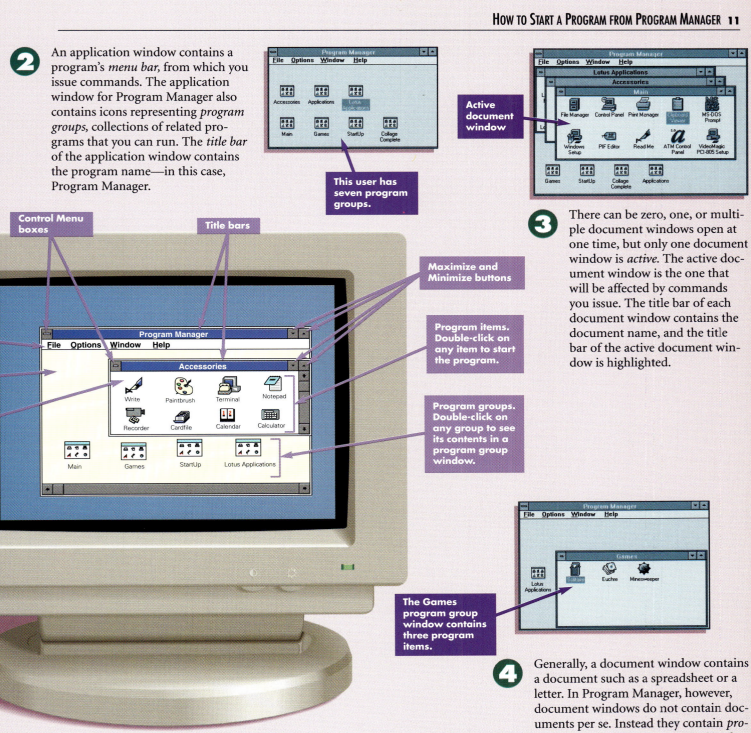

The Games program group window contains three program items.

4 Generally, a document window contains a document such as a spreadsheet or a letter. In Program Manager, however, document windows do not contain documents per se. Instead they contain *program items,* little icons representing the programs within a program group. The fact that the window is called a "document window" is a quirk of Windows terminology. For clarity, document windows in Program Manager are usually called *program group windows.*

Double-click to open the Accessories program group window.

How to Use the Mouse in Windows

An *input device* is a means of giving instructions to your computer. You're probably familiar with the keyboard as the most common input device. A *mouse,* so named for its hunched-over appearance and tail-like cable, is a hand-held input device that along with the keyboard is one of the two input devices most people use routinely in Windows. Although it's possible to get by without a mouse and do all your work from the keyboard, it's not too wise. The Windows interface was designed with the mouse in mind. Keyboard alternatives can be awkward—and it's not always easy to find out what they are. Take a few minutes to learn the major mouse moves and you'll reward yourself with smoother computing.

TIP SHEET

▶ Unless told otherwise, use the *left* mouse button. The other mouse button or buttons are used so infrequently in Windows that when they *are* used, you're always told about it specifically.

▶ Some mice have two buttons, and others have three. The right mouse button is used infrequently, and the middle button on the three-button mouse is almost never used.

▶ For keyboard alternatives to the scroll bars and the Maximize/Minimize/Restore buttons, turn the page.

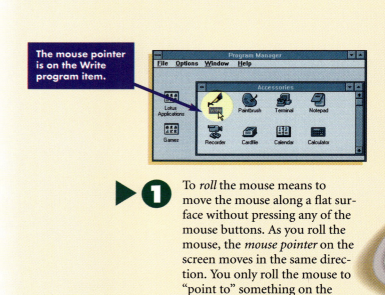

The mouse pointer is on the Write program item.

1 To *roll* the mouse means to move the mouse along a flat surface without pressing any of the mouse buttons. As you roll the mouse, the *mouse pointer* on the screen moves in the same direction. You only roll the mouse to "point to" something on the screen as a prelude to another action.

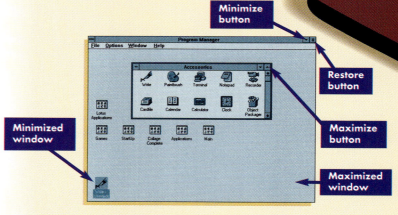

Minimize button

Restore button

Maximize button

Minimized window

Maximized window

6 To *maximize* a window (enlarge it so it fills the screen), click on its Maximize button. To *restore* a maximized window to its original size, click on its Restore button. To *minimize* a window so it's merely an icon with a title, click on its Minimize button. To restore a minimized window to its original size, double-click on its title or icon.

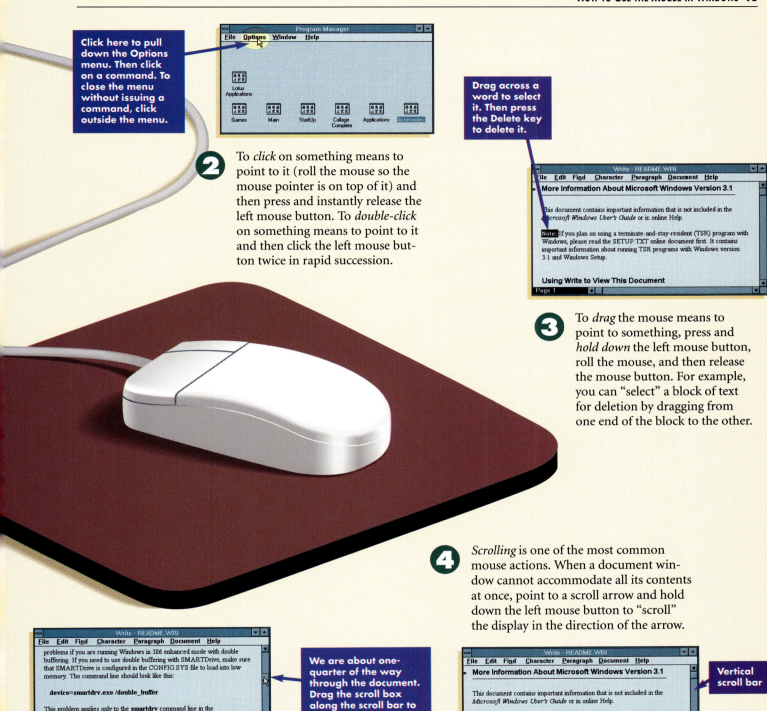

Click here to pull down the Options menu. Then click on a command. To close the menu without issuing a command, click outside the menu.

Drag across a word to select it. Then press the Delete key to delete it.

2 To *click* on something means to point to it (roll the mouse so the mouse pointer is on top of it) and then press and instantly release the left mouse button. To *double-click* on something means to point to it and then click the left mouse button twice in rapid succession.

3 To *drag* the mouse means to point to something, press and *hold down* the left mouse button, roll the mouse, and then release the mouse button. For example, you can "select" a block of text for deletion by dragging from one end of the block to the other.

4 *Scrolling* is one of the most common mouse actions. When a document window cannot accommodate all its contents at once, point to a scroll arrow and hold down the left mouse button to "scroll" the display in the direction of the arrow.

We are about one-quarter of the way through the document. Drag the scroll box along the scroll bar to see the rest of the document.

Vertical scroll bar

Horizontal scroll bar

5 Another way to scroll is to drag the scroll box to a new location along the scroll bar. The position of the scroll box suggests what part of the contents you are viewing.

Point here and hold down the left mouse button to scroll down through the document.

How to Use the Keyboard in Windows

In Windows and in most Windows-based programs, you don't have to use the keyboard for much of anything—except, of course, to type text. But if you type quite a bit, you may be interested in optional ways to issue commands, move through documents such as spreadsheets, and perform other common actions without having to reach for the mouse. The more experience you get in a Windows-based program, the more likely you'll hanker for keyboard alternatives to the mouse actions you perform most often. Even if you're a true mouse-o-phile, you should be aware of the major keyboard techniques in case your mouse ever malfunctions.

1 The Shift, Alt, and Ctrl keys work in combination with other keys. No doubt you know that pressing the Shift key along with a letter key types a capital letter. Shift, Alt, and Ctrl can combine with practically any key on your keyboard.

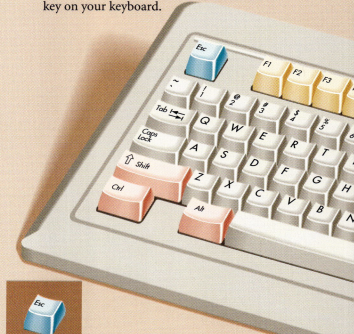

TIP SHEET

▶ In many programs, the Page Up and Page Down keys scroll the window contents in large increments, Ctrl+Home moves to the top of the window contents, and Ctrl+End moves to the bottom. (Ctrl+End doesn't work in 1-2-3, though.)

▶ Your function keys may be across the top of the keyboard or along the left side. Function keys along the side are easier for touch typists to reach and may make it worthwhile to memorize some keyboard shortcuts in your favorite programs.

7 Not surprisingly, the Escape key (Esc on most keyboards) lets you slam the door on possible hazards. If you pull down a menu but decide not to issue a command, press Escape twice to close the menu and deactivate the menu bar. If you issue a command and a dialog box appears (see next page) but you don't want to proceed, press Escape to close the dialog box.

6 To pull down a menu from the menu bar, press Alt and then type the underlined character in the menu name. For example, in Program Manager press Alt and type **o** to pull down the Options menu. Then, to issue a command from the menu, type the underlined character in the command name.

2 Shift, Alt, and Ctrl often combine with the *function keys*, labeled F1 through F10 or F12, as an alternative way to issue a command. For example, in most Windows programs, press Alt+F4 (hold down Alt, press and release F4, and release Alt) to close the program.

3 When you don't want to reach for the mouse to scroll through the contents of a window, use the ↑, ↓, →, and ← *arrow keys* instead. Some keyboards have a separate set of arrow keys, while others have only the arrow keys on the numeric keypad. If the arrows on the numeric keypad don't work, press the Num Lock key and they should work fine.

4 Press the Caps Lock key to type a series of uppercase letters without holding down Shift, and press Caps Lock again to switch it off when you're done typing in uppercase. Press the Num Lock key to use the numeric keypad for typing numbers rather than for scrolling, and press Num Lock again to switch off this feature.

Type the underlined character to issue the command.

Control menu of the Accessories document window

5 To maximize, minimize, restore, or close a window, first open its Control menu. Press Alt+spacebar to open the Control menu of an application window; press Alt+hyphen to open the Control menu of a document window. Use the ↓ key to highlight the command you want: Maximize, Minimize, Restore, or Close. Then press Enter.

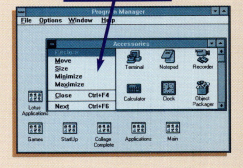

How to Talk to a Dialog Box

A *dialog box* is where you give Windows (or a Windows-based program) the information it needs to carry out a command you have issued. Say you issue a command called Print, a command found in many programs. Before doing any printing, the program may present a dialog box to ask you how much of the window contents to print, how many copies to print, what printer to print it on, and so forth. Once you answer, the Print command takes effect. The name *dialog box* is slightly misleading. In a human dialog, the participants take turns speaking. In a computerized dialog, the program asks all its questions at once, and then you give all your answers. It's more like a questionnaire than a dialog.

TIP SHEET

▶ **To choose a dialog box option from the keyboard, hold down Alt and type the underlined character in the option name. If the dialog box lacks underlined characters, press Tab to move from option to option. Then, to mark or clear a check box, press the spacebar. To mark the desired radio button within a group, use the arrow keys. To drop down a list, press the down arrow key; then press the down arrow to highlight your choice, and press Tab. (These conventions are followed in most, but not all, Windows applications.)**

▶ **If you need to see what's behind a dialog box, move the box by dragging its title bar.**

▶ **To close a dialog box without issuing the command, click on the Cancel button (available in most dialog boxes), double-click on the box's Control Menu box, or press Escape.**

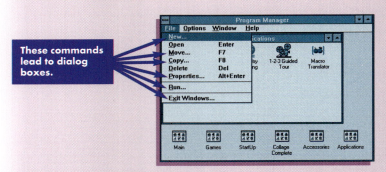

These commands lead to dialog boxes.

1 In Windows menus, the presence of three dots after a command name means that a dialog box will appear when you issue the command. Some dialog boxes are small while others take up most of the screen. It depends on how many questions the program needs to ask.

OK

6 When you've provided all the information requested, issue the command by clicking on the button labeled OK or on another appropriately named button. (The button name might be Print or Find or something else related to the command.)

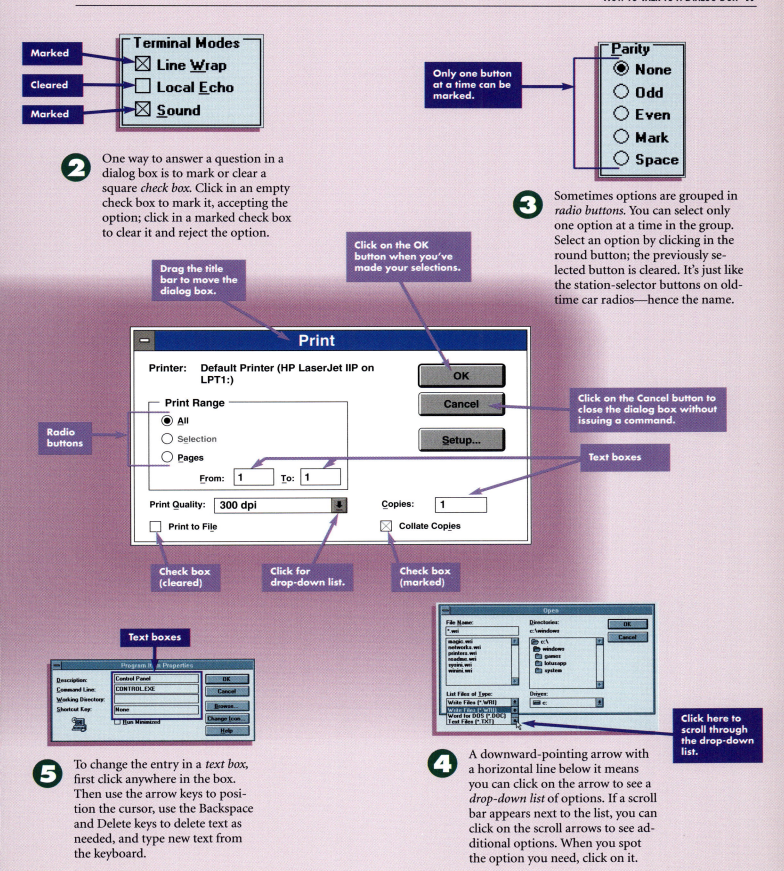

Marked

Cleared

Marked

Terminal Modes
- ☒ Line Wrap
- ☐ Local Echo
- ☒ Sound

Only one button at a time can be marked.

Parity
- ◉ None
- ○ Odd
- ○ Even
- ○ Mark
- ○ Space

2 One way to answer a question in a dialog box is to mark or clear a square *check box.* Click in an empty check box to mark it, accepting the option; click in a marked check box to clear it and reject the option.

3 Sometimes options are grouped in *radio buttons.* You can select only one option at a time in the group. Select an option by clicking in the round button; the previously selected button is cleared. It's just like the station-selector buttons on old-time car radios—hence the name.

Drag the title bar to move the dialog box.

Click on the OK button when you've made your selections.

Print

Printer: Default Printer (HP LaserJet IIP on LPT1:)

Radio buttons

Print Range
- ◉ All
- ○ Selection
- ○ Pages

From: 1   To: 1

OK

Cancel

Setup...

Click on the Cancel button to close the dialog box without issuing a command.

Text boxes

Print Quality: 300 dpi

Copies: 1

☐ Print to File   ☒ Collate Copies

Check box (cleared)

Click for drop-down list.

Check box (marked)

Text boxes

Program Item Properties

Description: Control Panel
Command Line: CONTROL.EXE
Working Directory:
Shortcut Key: None
☐ Run Minimized

OK
Cancel
Browse...
Change Icon...
Help

Open

File Name:
*.wri

magic.wri
networks.wri
printers.wri
readme.wri
sysini.wri
winini.wri

Directories:
c:\windows

📁 c:\
📁 windows
📁 games
📁 lotusapp
📁 system

OK
Cancel

List Files of Type:
Write Files (*.WRI)
Write Files (*.WRI)
Word for DOS (*.DOC)
Text Files (*.TXT)

Drivers:
💾 c:

Click here to scroll through the drop-down list.

5 To change the entry in a *text box,* first click anywhere in the box. Then use the arrow keys to position the cursor, use the Backspace and Delete keys to delete text as needed, and type new text from the keyboard.

4 A downward-pointing arrow with a horizontal line below it means you can click on the arrow to see a *drop-down list* of options. If a scroll bar appears next to the list, you can click on the scroll arrows to see additional options. When you spot the option you need, click on it.

CHAPTER 3

Welcome to 1-2-3

1-2-3 operations are based on worksheets and worksheet files. A *worksheet* is the basic spreadsheet, like a page from an old-fashioned ledger book. It is where you enter and work with related data. A *worksheet file* is like the ledger book itself: a set of worksheets. You will find it convenient to keep related worksheets—for example, all your company's personnel worksheets—in one worksheet file.

When you start 1-2-3 for Windows, you have the choice of working with a new, blank worksheet file or opening an existing worksheet file that contains data you entered previously.

Though no data is displayed when you start 1-2-3, your screen is not exactly blank. Rather, it contains an array of tools designed to help you work. Some of these tools, such as the Control Menu boxes, menu bar, and scroll bars, are common to most Windows-based programs. Others are particular to 1-2-3.

As you progress through this book, you will take advantage of many of these tools in your work. Other tools are so specialized that you may never use them (and never miss them). One key to learning 1-2-3 painlessly is to be undaunted by the large number of tools available. This book will point out the most important tools when you need them. Blissfully ignore the rest.

This chapter briefly introduces you to the environment you'll call home when using 1-2-3. Relax and take a little time to get your bearings.

How to Get Started in 1-2-3

When you start 1-2-3 for Windows, you see a maximized application window that contains a maximized document window. These windows together make up the three parts of the 1-2-3 screen: the *control panel*, the *work area*, and the *status bar*. This page describes these three areas and their elements.

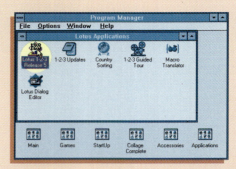

▶**1** To start 1-2-3, first start Windows. Then open the Lotus Applications program group (or whichever program group contains your 1-2-3 program items) and double-click on the Lotus 1-2-3 Release 5 program item (See Chapter 2 for help with these operations.)

▶ **If you don't want to see the Welcome to 1-2-3 dialog box shown in step 2 every time you start 1-2-3, check Don't show this screen again before clicking on Cancel.**

▶ **If your opening screen differs from the ones shown here, you may wish to reset certain display options so you can better follow the instructions and examples in this book. To do this, click on View in the menu bar and then click on the Set View Preferences command. In the Set View Preferences dialog box that opens next, make sure that every check box is marked and that the Custom zoom % text box is set to 87. Then click on OK. Don't worry about other differences between your screen and the ones shown in this book. They shouldn't affect your ability to learn and use 1-2-3.**

▶ **What you see in the data area when you start 1-2-3 is only the top-left corner of the current worksheet. Each 1-2-3 worksheet contains 256 columns and 8,192 rows for a total of 2,097,152 cells!**

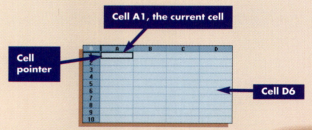

Cell A1, the current cell

Cell pointer

Cell D6

7 Each intersection of a column and row forms a single *cell*. As indicated by the column letters and row numbers, 1-2-3 refers to each cell by a unique letter-number designation, called a *cell address*. For example, the cell where column D and row 6 intersect is cell D6. The *current cell*—that is, the cell that will be affected by actions you take—is indicated by a thick outline called the *cell pointer*.

6 Take a closer look at the data area. Along the bottom and right edges are scroll bars to help you move through your worksheet (see Chapter 5). *Column letters* line the top edge of the data area, and *row numbers* line the left edge. The center of the data area contains a series of vertical *columns* and horizontal *rows*.

2 Depending on your computer's setup, you may see the Welcome to 1-2-3 dialog box, which is designed to help you create and open worksheet files. Because we'll be showing you how to do just these things in this book, just click on Cancel if necessary to bypass this dialog box.

3 The *control panel* sits along the top of your screen and consists of three elements: the title bar, the menu bar, and the edit line. The *title bar* currently shows you that you're running Lotus 1-2-3 Release 5 with an untitled worksheet file open; as you work in 1-2-3, the title bar often displays helpful messages about the task at hand. The *menu bar* contains eight menu names; each menu contains a set of 1-2-3 commands. The *edit line* contains various elements for entering and editing data, and for finding your way through worksheets.

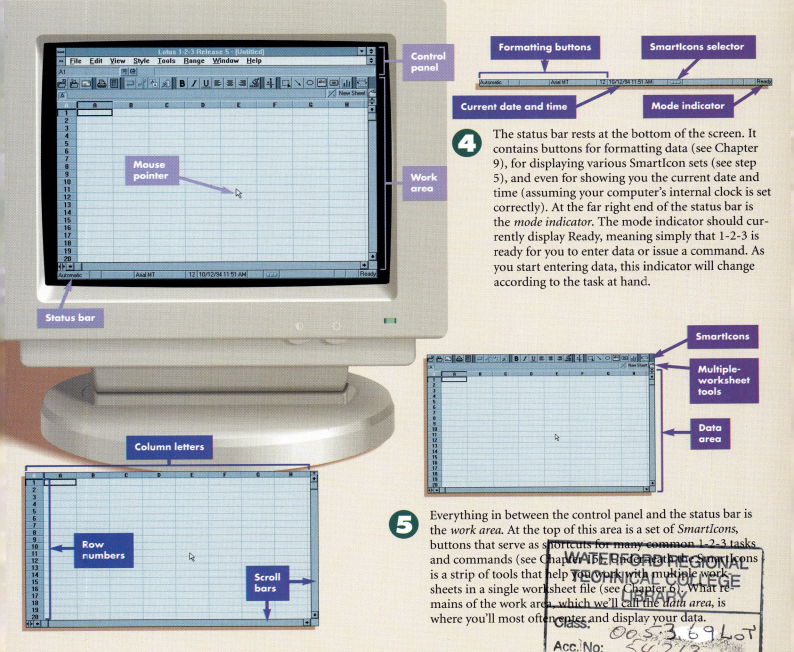

4 The status bar rests at the bottom of the screen. It contains buttons for formatting data (see Chapter 9), for displaying various SmartIcon sets (see step 5), and even for showing you the current date and time (assuming your computer's internal clock is set correctly). At the far right end of the status bar is the *mode indicator*. The mode indicator should currently display Ready, meaning simply that 1-2-3 is ready for you to enter data or issue a command. As you start entering data, this indicator will change according to the task at hand.

5 Everything in between the control panel and the status bar is the *work area*. At the top of this area is a set of *SmartIcons*, buttons that serve as shortcuts for many common 1-2-3 tasks and commands (see Chapter 15). Underneath the SmartIcons is a strip of tools that help you work with multiple worksheets in a single worksheet file (see Chapter 6). What remains of the work area, which we'll call the *data area*, is where you'll most often enter and display your data.

CHAPTER 4

Setting Up a Worksheet

A worksheet file containing vital business data is bound to be part of your life for a long time. Therefore, you should plan the structure of each worksheet carefully. A well-planned, well-structured worksheet saves you time and aggravation in two ways. First, it makes data easy to find and use. And second, it saves you time you might spend restructuring the worksheet later.

What is involved in planning a worksheet? Fundamentally, not much. Decide what data you need to present, what order to present it in, and what operations to perform on it. Beneath this fundamental simplicity, however, may rest layers of complexity that only you, as the holder of the business data, can fathom. After a few months, today's perfect worksheet may look like a relic from the Dark Ages as accounting codes are revised, departments are added, new reports are requested, and employees come and go.

The upshot: Take some time to think about your data needs before firing up 1-2-3. Then build your worksheet. This chapter is here to help you get started and make minor changes to your data. What about those inevitable overhauls down the road? 1-2-3 makes them quite painless. The techniques you'll need are covered in Chapter 8.

How to Enter Data

Anytime the mode indicator at the right end of your status bar displays *Ready*, you can enter data in your worksheet. You enter data simply by typing letters, numbers, and punctuation marks on your keyboard. The procedure is the same whether you are entering text (such as a column heading) or numbers.

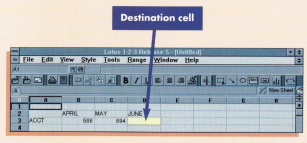

Destination cell

▶ **1** Locate the cell where you want to insert data. Use the scroll bars to scroll the cell into view if it is hidden.

TIP SHEET

▶ You can also enter data in the current cell (step 4) *and* move to an adjacent cell in one step by pressing one of your keyboard's arrow keys.

▶ 1-2-3 lets you enter data that is too wide for the column. This data may appear to spill over into an adjacent column, or 1-2-3 may not display the data completely. Regardless of the display, 1-2-3 "remembers" your complete entry and restores its display if you widen the column (see Chapter 8). If the entry is a number, 1-2-3 will use the complete number in calculations even if the display is incomplete.

▶ See Chapter 5 to learn how to edit cell contents after entering them.

▶ 1-2-3 automatically left-aligns numbers and right-aligns text within each cell. (If the data is a mixture of text and numbers, 1-2-3 uses left alignment.) See Chapter 9 to learn how to change cell alignment.

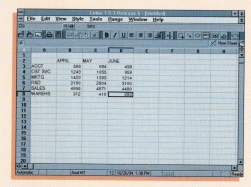

6 Once you've entered data for one cell, the mode indicator once again displays *Ready*, indicating that 1-2-3 is ready for you to enter more data. Repeat the preceding steps to enter the rest of your data.

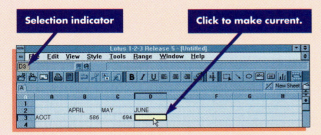

Selection indicator

Click to make current.

2 Click in the cell to make it the current cell. Or use your keyboard's ↑, ↓, ←, or → arrow keys to move the cell pointer to the desired cell. The current cell's address displays in the edit line's *selection indicator*.

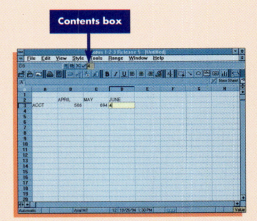

Contents box

3 Type the cell contents. What you type appears both in the current cell and in the edit line's *contents box*. Observe that when you start typing, the mode indicator changes from *Ready* to *Value* (if you type numbers) or *Label* (if you type letters).

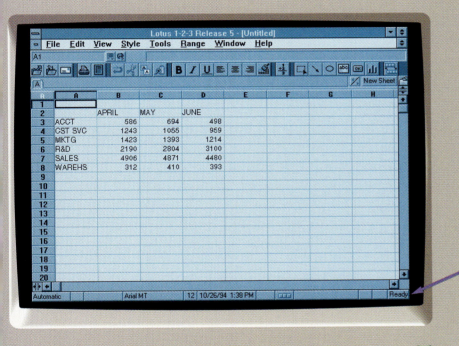

1-2-3 is ready to accept data.

4 When you're done typing in the current cell, click on the edit line's *Confirm button*. Or simply press the Enter key on your keyboard. This is called *entering* the data.

Confirm button

Cancel button

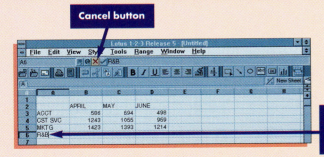

Press Backspace once for each character you want to delete.

5 If you make a mistake while typing your data (but before entering it), press the Backspace key one or more times as necessary to delete the last character or characters. Or, to erase everything in the cell and start over, click on the edit line's *Cancel button* or press the Escape (Esc) key on your keyboard.

How to Enter a Formula

Much of the "magic" of electronic spreadsheets is that a cell need not contain fixed data. Instead, a cell can contain a *formula* that displays the result of a calculation performed on data stored in *other* cells. If you later edit the data in those other cells (see Chapter 5), the displayed result changes automatically.

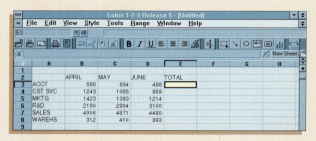

1 Move the cell pointer to the cell where you want to place the formula. (Use the arrow keys or click in the cell.)

TIP SHEET

▶ **You can also start formulas (step 2) with a number or any of the following characters: -, =, (, @, ., $, or #. Because some of these characters have special functions, though, you should probably avoid them until you learn more about 1-2-3. (Turn the page to see the @ character in use.)**

▶ **You cannot tell just by looking at a worksheet whether a cell contains a fixed number or the results of a formula. Instead, you must make the cell current and then look at the contents box.**

▶ **1-2-3 never miscalculates. If the result of a formula is obviously wrong, or if 1-2-3 presents an error message, then you typed the formula incorrectly. Common mistakes include forgetting the leading plus sign, mistyping a cell reference, and including spaces in a formula. See Chapter 5 to learn how to edit a formula.**

▶ **In cell references, you can type letters in uppercase or lowercase. 1-2-3 converts the letters to uppercase when you enter the formula.**

5 The cell now displays the calculated result of your formula. Whenever the cell is current, though, the edit line's contents box displays the underlying formula.

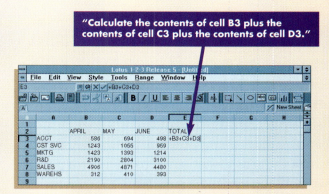

"Calculate the contents of cell B3 plus the contents of cell C3 plus the contents of cell D3."

2 Type a plus sign (+). (Your keyboard has two + keys; use either one.) This tells 1-2-3 to treat the data that follows as a formula.

3 Using no spaces, type the calculation you want to perform. Where appropriate, use *cell references*—that is, cell addresses—instead of the actual numbers stored in the referenced cells. That way, if you later revise the numbers in the referenced cells, 1-2-3 will redo the calculation based on the new numbers. The mathematical operators available in formulas include + for addition, – for subtraction, ˣ for multiplication, / for division, and ^ for exponentiation.

Formula

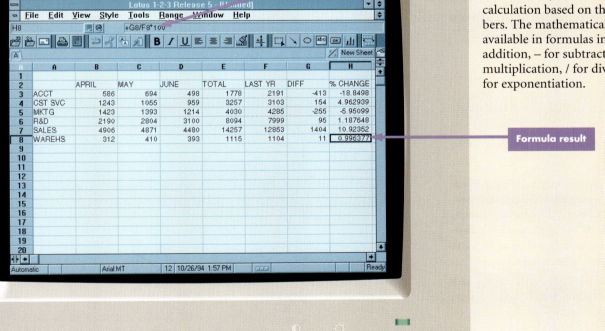

Formula result

4 Enter the formula by clicking on the Confirm button, pressing the Enter key, or pressing one of the arrow keys.

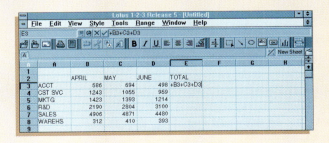

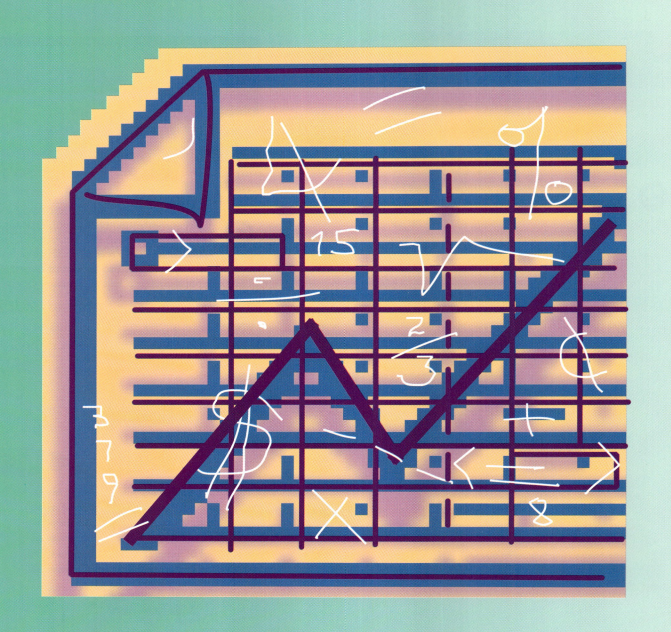

CHAPTER 5

Working with Worksheets

 You don't build a worksheet just to look at it; a worksheet is a *tool*. It helps you understand your business data, forecast the future, and make decisions.

Using a worksheet requires skills beyond the data and formula entry you've learned so far. What happens when your data changes? What if you need to project the impact of possible future data? What about whole new data types—a new department, revised accounting codes, personnel changes?

Anyone who uses an electronic spreadsheet needs certain worksheet maintenance skills. This chapter covers the most fundamental of those skills. In this chapter you will learn how to find your way around a large worksheet, how to edit data, how to project future results ("what-if" analysis), and how to select a group of cells so that you can apply a command to all of them. Future chapters expand and reinforce these important techniques.

How to Move through a Worksheet

Rarely is a worksheet compact enough to fit on the screen all at once. Many 1-2-3 worksheets sprawl across dozens of columns and hundreds of rows. For example, a personnel worksheet may contain pay and benefits information for hundreds or even thousands of employees. A worksheet with a company's financial figures may cover several years, month by month. You already know that you can scroll any part of the worksheet into view and then click in any cell to make it current, or simply move into a cell using the arrow keys. But there are easier, more efficient ways to move about a large worksheet. Here are the best of them.

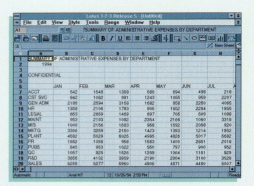

▶ ① To move to cell A1, press Home.

⑦ Finally, click on the OK button. The cell you named becomes the current cell.

Some rows are out of view.

⑥ Next, in the Go To dialog box's only text box, type the address of the cell to which you want to move.

TIP SHEET

▶ Scrolling with the scroll bars does not change the current cell. Therefore, it is possible for the current cell to be out of view. Even in this situation, the edit line's selection indicator tells you the current cell.

▶ The bottom-right cell in the active area of the worksheet (step 2) is the intersection of the last nonblank row and the last nonblank column in the worksheet. Depending on the worksheet structure, this may be a blank cell.

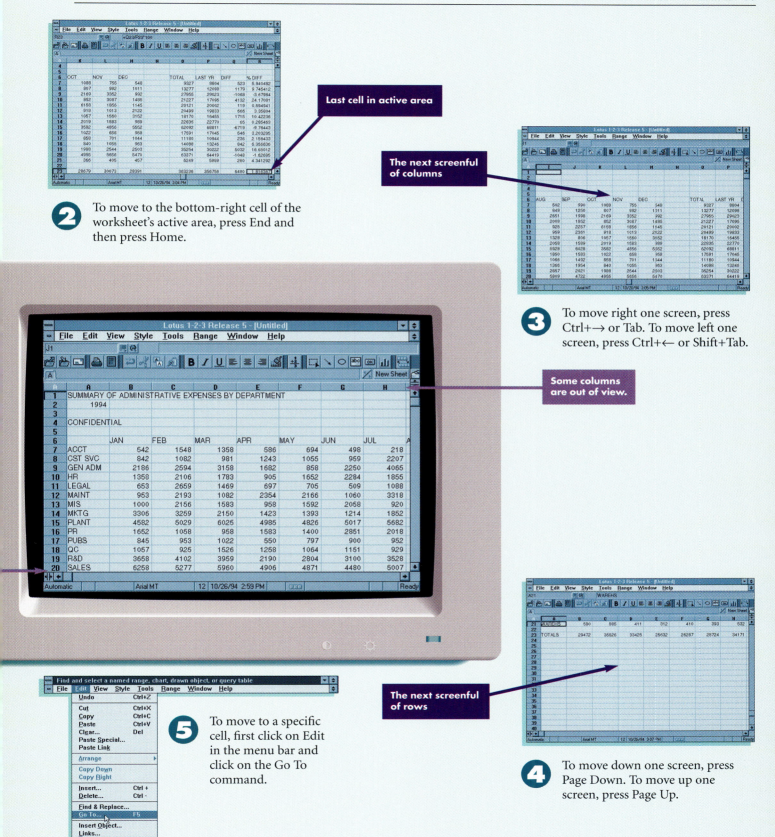

Last cell in active area

2 To move to the bottom-right cell of the worksheet's active area, press End and then press Home.

The next screenful of columns

3 To move right one screen, press Ctrl+→ or Tab. To move left one screen, press Ctrl+← or Shift+Tab.

Some columns are out of view.

5 To move to a specific cell, first click on Edit in the menu bar and click on the Go To command.

The next screenful of rows

4 To move down one screen, press Page Down. To move up one screen, press Page Up.

How to Edit Cell Contents

There are many reasons to *edit* (change) the contents of cells in a worksheet: to correct a misspelling in a text entry, to revise data, or to fix an incorrect formula, for example. The way you edit cell contents is the same whether the cell contains text, numbers, or a formula (see Chapter 4).

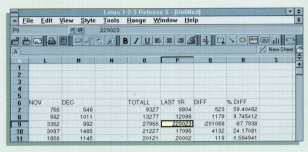

▶ ❶ Move the cell pointer to the cell you want to edit.

Recalculated formula

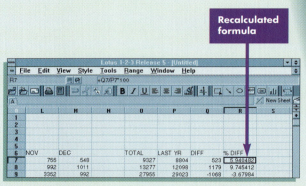

❻ Observe that 1-2-3 recalculates a formula as soon as you edit it and displays the new result in the cell.

❺ Finally, click on the Confirm button, press Enter, or press one of the ↑ or ↓ arrow keys.

2 To completely replace the cell contents, simply type the new contents and then click on the Confirm button, press Enter, or press one of the arrow keys. It's the same as typing into a blank cell.

When you edit data, any formulas or functions relying on that data are recalculated automatically.

Insertion point

3 To modify rather than replace the cell contents, first double-click in the cell. A flashing insertion point in the cell tells you that the cell is ready for editing. (Notice also that the mode indicator now displays *Edit*.) If the cell contains a formula, that formula—rather than the formula's result—is now displayed.

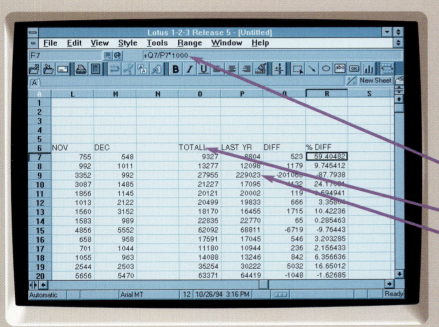

Incorrect formula

Misspelling

Data entry error

Press Backspace to delete one character to the left of the insertion point. Press Delete to delete one character to the right.

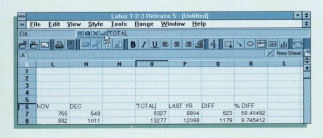

4 Next, using the typing keys, the ← and → arrow keys, Delete, and/or Backspace, type and delete characters as needed to modify the cell contents. (When you're editing a cell, the ← and → arrow keys move you left and right within a cell rather than from cell to cell.)

How to Ask "What If?"

What-if analysis is the testing of the impact of sample data. What if the bank reduces the loan rate by one percent? What if our utility bills go up by four thousand dollars next quarter? What if the new salesperson brings in two million dollars in new business next year? What-if analysis in 1-2-3 instantly shows you the results of scenarios like these. All you have to do is insert your estimated data in a worksheet and let 1-2-3's automatic recalculation work its magic.

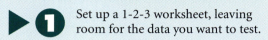

1 Set up a 1-2-3 worksheet, leaving room for the data you want to test.

▶ **Rather than insert and replace your sample values to test their impact, it is also possible to set up several sections in your worksheet, each section identical except for the sample data it contains. Then you can view the potential results of different data simultaneously. Setting up nearly identical sections in a worksheet will be easier once you know how to copy data, as explained in Chapter 8.**

▶ **Playing "what if" may involve inserting new columns and rows into your existing data. Chapter 8 explains how.**

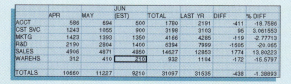

6 Repeat steps 4 and 5 until you have tested as many sample values as you need.

2 Enter the sample data the same way you enter any data in a 1-2-3 worksheet.

JUN
(EST)

650
1150
1400
2500

	APR	MAY	JUN (EST)	TOTAL	LAST YR	DIFF	% DIFF
ACCT	586	694	650	1930	2191	-261	-11.9124
CST SVC	1243	1055	1150	3448	3103	345	11.11827
MKTG	1423	1393	1400	4216	4285	-69	-1.61027
R&D	2190	2804	2500	7494	7999	-505	-6.31329
SALES	4906	4871	4890	14667	12853	1814	14.11344
WAREHS	312	410	350	1072	1104	-32	-2.89855
TOTALS	10660	11227	10940	32827	31535	1292	4.097035

3 Observe the results in cells that contain formulas referencing the sample data. You may wish to write down the results or print them (see Chapter 7) so you can compare them with the results obtained from other data estimates.

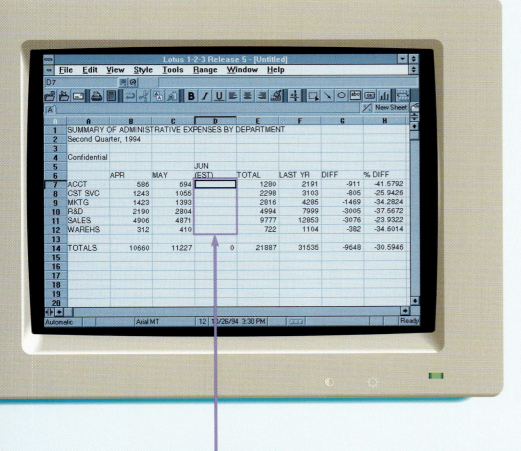

JUN
(EST)

800
1400
1450
2500
4890
350

4 Replace the sample data with new data (as explained on the preceding page).

Plug in various possible June results and see how they affect the totals and differences.

	APR	MAY	JUN (EST)	TOTAL	LAST YR	DIFF	% DIFF
ACCT	586	694	800	2080	2191	-111	-5.06618
CST SVC	1243	1055	1400	3698	3103	595	19.17499
MKTG	1423	1393	1450	4266	4285	-19	-0.44341
R&D	2190	2804	2500	7494	7999	-505	-6.31329
SALES	4906	4871	4890	14667	12853	1814	14.11344
WAREHS	312	410	350	1072	1104	-32	-2.89855
TOTALS	10660	11227	11390	33277	31535	1742	5.524021

5 Again observe the results and compare them with the results obtained before.

How to Select Ranges and Collections

A *range* is a rectangular group of adjacent cells that you *select* (highlight) so that you can issue commands affecting all the cells at once. Nonrectangular and/or nonadjacent cell groups are known instead as *collections*, but they serve the same purpose. In "How to Sum Numbers" (Chapter 4), you learned how to define a range or collection by typing cell references manually. In this and many other cases, you can instead define a range or collection by selecting it right on the worksheet. This not only saves you typing time, but can also increase the accuracy of your formulas. This page shows you how to select ranges and collections; future chapters cover many of the advantages of doing so.

1 To select a range, first position the mouse pointer over one of the end or corner cells that define the desired range.

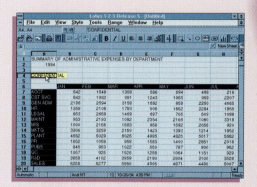

6 To add a single cell to your selection, click on that cell while holding down Ctrl.

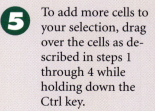

5 To add more cells to your selection, drag over the cells as described in steps 1 through 4 while holding down the Ctrl key.

Notice the mouse pointer's shape.

② Making sure the mouse pointer appears as a plain, left-pointing arrow, hold down the left mouse button and start dragging to the opposite end or corner of the range. As you start dragging, your mouse pointer changes shape to show you that you are successfully selecting a range.

Even though it may not look like it, the current cell is part of the selection.

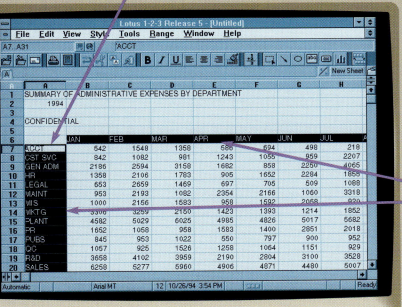

These two ranges comprise a collection.

③ Cells are selected (highlighted) as you pass over them. Don't worry if part of the range is out of view. 1-2-3 will scroll the display automatically when you drag to the edge of the data area.

④ When the opposite cell in your range becomes selected, release the mouse button. The cells remain highlighted, defining your range. If 1-2-3 automatically scrolled to accommodate your selection, it will automatically scroll back to show the beginning of the range. If you need to select a collection, continue on to step 5; otherwise, skip the remaining steps.

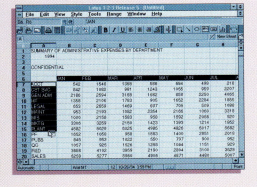

The selection indicator displays the current range address.

CHAPTER 6

Worksheet File Access

Just like the business it supports, a worksheet file can take on a life of its own. Data are updated, new formulas are required, colleagues request information—a worksheet file can be with you for months or even years.

Unfortunately, you cannot casually switch off your computer and hope to return to an unsullied worksheet file later. Computers require special procedures for storing data and returning to it. Follow these procedures and you can safely take a break from your work, confident that your 1-2-3 worksheet files will be available whenever you want to come back to them.

This chapter covers an array of features collectively called *worksheet file access*. It explains how to save a worksheet file, remove it from the screen, and exit and restart 1-2-3. It also shows you how to start a new worksheet file *without* exiting and restarting 1-2-3, how to reopen a saved worksheet file, and how to use multiple worksheets within a single worksheet file. These techniques are among the most fundamental you'll learn in this book, and many of the concepts behind them apply to almost any computer program you'll ever use.

How to Save and Close a Worksheet File

As you enter data into 1-2-3, that data exists only in your computer's memory (RAM), a rather precarious storage area. RAM is no place to keep something you plan to use later—such as an important or incomplete worksheet file. If your worksheet file is even remotely important and if there is any chance that you'll want to come back to it later, you should *save* it on a disk. After saving a worksheet file, you can continue working on it, or you can close it and then either work on another worksheet file or exit 1-2-3 (see the next three pages).

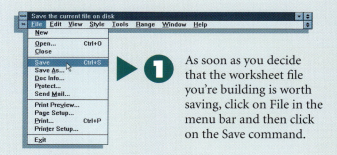

1 As soon as you decide that the worksheet file you're building is worth saving, click on File in the menu bar and then click on the Save command.

TIP SHEET

▶ **If your computer loses power or otherwise malfunctions, you'll lose whatever is in RAM. On disk, though, you'll still have your worksheet file exactly as it was last time you saved it. After restarting your computer, you can open the file from disk and continue working on it. (See "How to Open a Worksheet File from Disk" later in this chapter.)**

▶ **Each disk or drive on your computer system is assigned a letter. Drive A usually refers to the disk in your first (and maybe only) floppy-disk drive. If your computer has two floppy-disk drives, drive B is usually the lower or rightmost of the two. Drive C is your hard-disk drive. Any drives higher than C are either network drives or additional areas of your hard disk.**

▶ **To save your worksheet file with a more meaningful description than a file name alone allows, type that description in the Save As dialog box's Comments box before clicking on OK in step 6.**

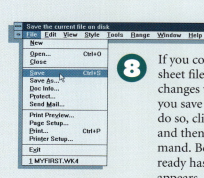

8 If you continue editing your worksheet file after saving it, your changes won't be saved on disk until you save the worksheet file again. To do so, click on File in the menu bar and then click on the Save command. Because the worksheet file already has a name, no dialog box appears. The revised worksheet file is saved and you can either close the worksheet file or continue working.

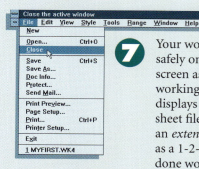

7 Your worksheet file is now stored safely on disk, but it remains on the screen as well so you can continue working on it. The title bar now displays the newly assigned worksheet file name, along with *.WK4*—an *extension* that identifies the file as a 1-2-3 worksheet file. If you're done working on this worksheet file for now, close it by clicking on File in the menu bar and then clicking on the Close command.

2 The Save As dialog box opens. Type a name for the worksheet file. (The File name text box is already active, and 1-2-3 suggests something like file0001.WK4 as the worksheet file name. Typing your own file name overwrites this suggestion.) A worksheet file name can contain up to eight characters; case is irrelevant. Spaces and the characters ?*."/|[]:|<>+=:, are not permitted in worksheet file names.

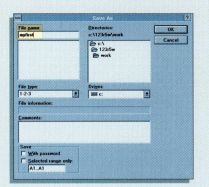

3 Observe the Directories entry in the dialog box. It displays the disk (drive) and directory where your computer will store your worksheet file unless you specify otherwise. (A *directory* is a division of a disk. Usually a directory contains related data and programs. Most hard disks and network disks have multiple directories, but many floppy disks do not.) If this location is okay, skip the next two steps.

4 To store the worksheet file on a different disk (drive), open the Drives drop-down list (click on the drop-down arrow to the right of the box), locate the disk you want—using the scroll bar if necessary—and click on it.

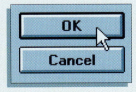

6 Click on the OK button to save the worksheet file under the specified name and in the specified location.

5 To store the worksheet file in a different directory, locate the directory name in the Directories list—using the scroll bar if necessary—and double-click on it. To see the subdirectories of any directory in the list, double-click on the directory name. (A *subdirectory* is a division of a directory—a directory *within* a directory, if you will.)

How to Start a New Worksheet File

Work does not come and go in neat little packets. As you build or edit one worksheet file, you may be called on to build or access another—pronto. You can start a new worksheet file anytime 1-2-3 is running—whether or not you have saved and closed the current worksheet file. This page shows you how.

Temporary worksheet name

1 One way to start a new worksheet file is to save and close every open worksheet (see preceding page). Once every other worksheet file is closed, 1-2-3 automatically creates a new, blank worksheet for you and gives your worksheet file the temporary name *Untitled*. You can skip to step 5.

6 If you used the New command to create your new worksheet file, other worksheet files might still be open—even if you can't see them. To switch back to another open worksheet file, click on Window in the menu bar and then click on the worksheet file's name.

2 If you'd prefer to keep some current worksheet files open instead, click on File in the menu bar and then click on the New command.

3 Depending on your 1-2-3 setup, you may see the New File dialog box. If so, verify that Create a plain worksheet is checked, and then click on OK.

4 A new, blank worksheet file appears, bearing the temporary name *FILE0001.WK4*, *FILE0002.WK4*, or something even higher.

5 Build, edit, save, and (optionally) close your new worksheet file.

How to Exit and Restart 1-2-3

It's wise to shut down 1-2-3 when you're done using it. Technically, it is not necessary to close one program before starting another. However, closing programs you're not using helps your computer run quicker and more efficiently. You'll also find it easier to use your computer under Windows if the only programs open are the ones you are using or plan to use in the very near future.

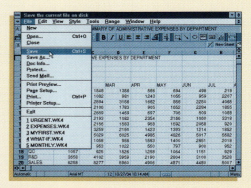

1 Save and close any open worksheet files that contain data (see preceding pages). Though 1-2-3 will remind you to save your worksheet files if you forget, taking the initiative to save your work is a good habit to form.

TIP SHEET

► Because 1-2-3 *always* displays some sort of worksheet file—blank or otherwise—figuring out what worksheet files are currently open can become confusing. Relax. Click on Window in the menu bar; the bottom of the menu will list every open worksheet file.

► You need not exit 1-2-3 just to use another Windows program briefly. Press Alt+Esc one or more times to switch among 1-2-3 and your other open Windows programs. For example, you can press Alt+Esc to switch to Program Manager, open another program, use it, (optionally) close it, and then press Alt+Esc until you are back in 1-2-3.

► If you try to exit Windows without closing 1-2-3 and you still have some unsaved worksheet files, 1-2-3 will give you a chance to save those files or exit Windows *without* saving.

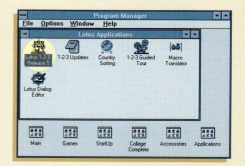

 Once back in Program Manager, you can restart 1-2-3 anytime by opening the program group window containing 1-2-3 and double-clicking on its program item (see Chapters 2 and 3).

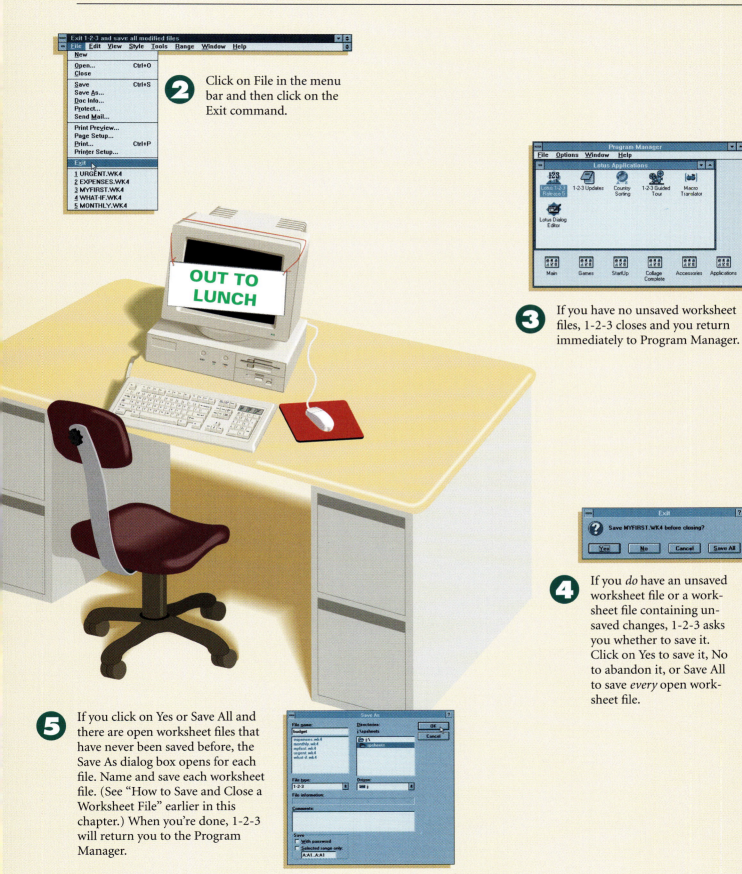

2 Click on File in the menu bar and then click on the Exit command.

3 If you have no unsaved worksheet files, 1-2-3 closes and you return immediately to Program Manager.

4 If you *do* have an unsaved worksheet file or a worksheet file containing unsaved changes, 1-2-3 asks you whether to save it. Click on Yes to save it, No to abandon it, or Save All to save *every* open worksheet file.

5 If you click on Yes or Save All and there are open worksheet files that have never been saved before, the Save As dialog box opens for each file. Name and save each worksheet file. (See "How to Save and Close a Worksheet File" earlier in this chapter.) When you're done, 1-2-3 will return you to the Program Manager.

How to Open a Worksheet File from Disk

The benefit of saving a worksheet file on disk is that you can later open (redisplay) it for reexamination or revision and then close it again when you're done. You can open an existing worksheet file anytime 1-2-3 is running, even if you haven't saved and closed the current worksheet file. This page shows you how.

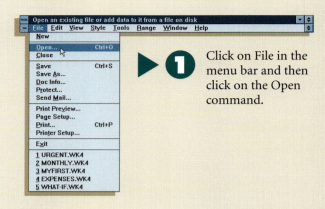

▶ **1** Click on File in the menu bar and then click on the Open command.

TIP SHEET

▶ If you open a worksheet file and change it, be sure to resave it so that your changes are stored on disk. Click on File in the menu bar and then click on the Save command.

▶ Sometimes it's useful to open a worksheet file, make some changes to it, and save it under a new name. That way you still have the original worksheet file available on disk under its original name. To do this, click on File in the menu bar, click on the Save As command, specify a worksheet file name and location, and then click on OK. Now your original worksheet file is stored safely away, and any changes affect the newly named worksheet file only.

▶ 1-2-3 offers a convenient way to open one of up to the last five worksheet files you've had open. Click on File in the menu bar and observe the list of file names at the bottom of the menu. If the worksheet file you want to open is listed there, simply click on it.

 The worksheet file appears on your screen, and its name is in the title bar. You are now free to edit the worksheet file.

2 In the Open File dialog box, observe the Directories entry. It displays the drive and directory where 1-2-3 is currently looking for worksheet files. If you've already saved or opened a file in the current work session, then 1-2-3 looks in that location. Otherwise, it looks in the *default* directory—1-2-3's preset location for worksheet files. If the worksheet file you want to open is in the current location, skip the next two steps.

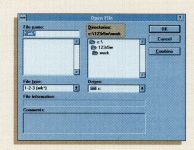

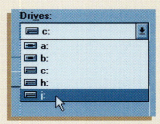

3 If your worksheet file is not on the current disk, open the Drives drop-down list, locate the disk containing the worksheet file—using the scroll bar if necessary—and click on it.

4 If your worksheet file is not in the current directory, locate the directory name in the Directories list—using the scroll bar if necessary—and double-click on it. To see the subdirectories of any directory in the list, double-click on the directory name.

5 In the File name list, locate the worksheet file you want to open—using the scroll bar if necessary—and double-click on it.

How to Work with Multiple Worksheets

You may want to keep several related worksheets (often called *sheets* for short) within one worksheet file, giving you faster access to related data. For example, you might keep one sheet for hourly-wage employees and a second sheet for salaried employees in one personnel worksheet file. Because keeping multiple worksheets in a single file makes it easy to include in one sheet a reference to data in another, you might also include a third sheet that combines figures from the other two sheets.

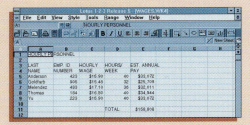

1 When you create a new worksheet file, it contains only one worksheet. This sheet is labeled *A* by default, as denoted by the *worksheet letter* at the intersection of the sheet's column letters and row numbers, and by the *worksheet tab* just above the worksheet letter.

TIP SHEET

▶ Even after you rename a worksheet, the worksheet *letter* remains the same (A, B, C, and so on). If you prefer, you can use these letters in formulas (see step 6) rather than typing out your customized worksheet names. When you enter those formulas, 1-2-3 will fill in the worksheet names automatically.

▶ If you create so many worksheets that you can no longer view all the worksheet tabs, use the *tab-scroll arrows*—located to the left of the New Sheet button—to scroll the tabs.

▶ You can alternately hide and display the worksheet tabs, tab-scroll arrows, and New Sheet button by clicking on the *Tab button*, located to the right of the New Sheet button.

▶ To delete a worksheet you no longer need, move to that sheet, click on Edit in the menu bar, click on the Delete command, click on Sheet in the Delete dialog box, and then click on OK.

"Calculate cell E11 from the Hourly worksheet plus cell D12 from the Salaried sheet."

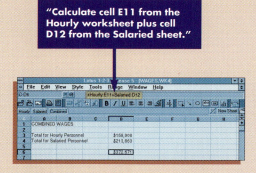

7 In a formula, reference a cell or range in another worksheet by preceding each cell reference or range with the worksheet name followed by a colon.

2 To create a new worksheet within the current worksheet file, click on the New Sheet button.

Worksheet tab

Worksheet letter

3 A new worksheet appears. Notice the worksheet letter and the new worksheet tab: The new sheet is labeled *B*. This new sheet provides you with a clean slate with which to work—just like turning to a new page in a paper ledger book. Enter and edit data and formulas in this new sheet as you would in any other.

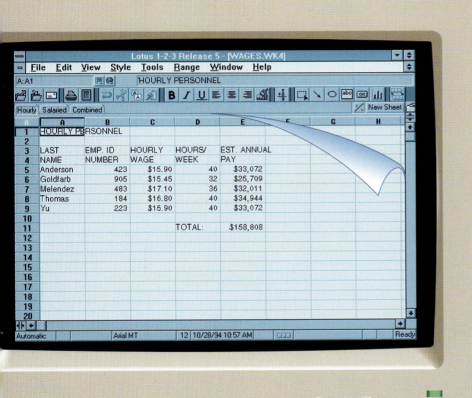

4 Repeat steps 2 and 3 as desired to create additional worksheets. Note that 1-2-3 places new sheets *after* the current one, so if you want to insert a new sheet between existing sheets A and B, for example, move to sheet A before clicking on the New Sheet button.

Double-click, type a name, and press Enter.

6 Although 1-2-3 by default labels worksheets A, B, C, and so on, it's smart to rename sheets to reflect their content. To do this, double-click on the appropriate worksheet tab, type a name, and then press Enter or click in the sheet. A worksheet name can be up to 15 characters long, and you can include spaces. However, don't start worksheet names with any of the characters !@$, and don't use the characters ,+<;:->.*@?/#&{=() anywhere in the name. Also, don't create worksheet names that look like cell addresses (such as A4 or J121).

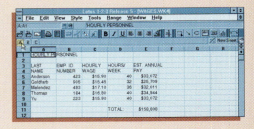

5 To move from one worksheet to another, click on the appropriate worksheet tab.

CHAPTER 7

Printing

 As long as the paperless office remains a fantasy, people will rely on printed documents as the primary way to share information.

1-2-3 joins forces with Windows and your printer to provide hassle-free worksheet printing. You can print your entire worksheet file, the current worksheet, or specific cells—quarterly figures, personnel records of one department, and so on.

By default, 1-2-3 gives you basic but good-looking printouts. It gives your data some breathing room by setting margins around the page, and it automatically splits larger worksheets across several pages as necessary.

If 1-2-3's basic defaults aren't good enough, though, you can customize your printouts by changing the default *Page Setup* options. For example, if your worksheet is too wide to fit on one page, you can choose to print it sideways (*landscape* orientation) rather than upright (*portrait* orientation). You can also ask 1-2-3 to shrink your data to make it fit. One important caveat: The customization options available to you may be limited by the abilities of your printer.

The next page explains how to print all or part of your worksheet file using 1-2-3's default Page Setup options. The page after that shows you several ways to customize those options.

How to Print All or Part of a Worksheet File

From any 1-2-3 worksheet file, you can print any range, collection, or worksheet, or you can choose to print the entire worksheet file. Note that when printing a worksheet or worksheet file, 1-2-3 prints only the active area of each sheet; that is, the rectangle-shaped group of cells whose top-left cell is cell A1 and stretches out to include every nonblank cell in that sheet. It does *not* print the usually vast empty spaces at the bottom and right of most worksheets.

TIP SHEET

▶ **If you print a collection, be aware that nonadjacent ranges in that collection may not print in the same relative positions they occupy on the worksheet. For example, if you select ranges in column A and column C, those ranges will print on top of one another rather than side by side.**

▶ **If your printout consists of more than one page, you can use the Pages options near the bottom of the Print dialog box to specify which pages you want 1-2-3 to print.**

▶ **To see how your printouts will look without actually printing them, click on Preview instead of on OK in step 6. Then, press the Escape key to return to your worksheet file. If you liked what you saw, just repeat the steps on this page. Otherwise, change the Page Setup options as described on the next page. Previewing your printouts can save a lot of paper and printer wear.**

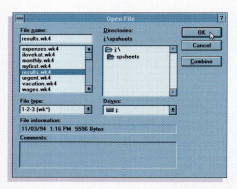

1 Open the worksheet file that contains the data you want to print.

7 1-2-3 informs you that it is sending your printer a copy of the worksheet file, worksheet, or selection. If you change your mind about printing the data, click on the Cancel button.

6 Make sure your printer is on and supplied with paper. Then, click on the OK button.

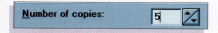

5 If you want to print more than one copy of your data, change the number in the Number of copies text box. To do this, either type over the existing number or click on the buttons to the right of the text box. Incredibly, you can print up to 9,999 copies. (For large volumes of printouts, though, it may be faster and less expensive to print one copy and photocopy the rest.)

2 If you want to print a specific range or collection of cells, select those cells. (See "How to Select Ranges and Collections" in Chapter 5.) If you want to print a specific worksheet, move to that worksheet.

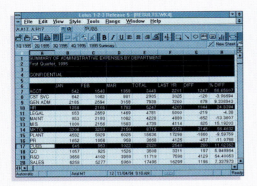

3 Click on File in the menu bar and then click on the Print command.

4 In the Print dialog box, click on the desired Print option: Current worksheet, All worksheets, or Selected range.

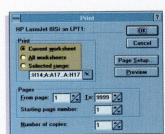

SUMMARY OF ADMINISTRATIVE EXPENSES BY DEPARTMENT
First Quarter, 1995

CONFIDENTIAL

	JAN	FEB	MAR	TOTAL	LAST YR	DIFF	% DIFF
ACCT	542	1548	1358	3448	2201	1247	56.65607
CST SVC	842	1082	981	2905	3025	-120	-3.96694
GEN ADM	2186	2594	3158	7938	7260	678	9.338843
HR	1358	2106	1783	5247	4203	1044	24.8394
LEGAL	653	2659	1469	4781	5000	-219	-4.38
MAINT	953	2193	1082	4228	4880	-652	-13.3607
MIS	1000	2156	1583	4739	4114	625	15.19203
MKTG	3306	3259	2150	8715	5570	3145	56.4632
PLANT	4582	5029	6025	15636	17296	-1660	-9.59759
PR	1652	1058	958	3668	4125	-457	-11.0788
PUBS	845	953	1022	2820	2540	280	11.02362
QC	1057	925	1526	3508	3311	197	5.949864
R&D	3658	4102	3959	11719	7590	4129	54.40053
SALES	6258	5277	5960	17495	16299	1196	7.337873
WAREHS	580	885	411	1876	1506	370	24.56839
TOTALS	29472	35826	33425	98723	88920	9803	11.02452

How to Improve Your Printouts

Although 1-2-3 does a decent job of printing data on its own, you may find many of your printouts somewhat lacking. For example, you may want to fit an otherwise multiple-page printout on one page, or center a small set of data on the page rather than having it stuck in the top-left corner. Perhaps you want to make your data easier to read by printing the on-screen *grid lines* that separate cells. And maybe you want to print important information such as the date, page number, and file name on each page. This page shows you how to improve your printouts by changing Page Setup options.

TIP SHEET

- ► This page explains how to improve printouts by changing Page Setup options. There are also several ways to improve the appearance of the text itself. For example, you can boldface text, and you can align column headings with the data below them. See Chapter 9 for details.

- ► The Fit all to page setting (step 3) can produce very tiny text. Depending on the data you're printing, you may instead want to choose Fit columns to page, which shrinks only columns, Fit rows to page, which shrinks only rows, or Manually scale, which enables you to shrink or expand your data anywhere from 15 to 1,000 percent of its original size. If none of these settings suits you, you can return to the default by choosing Actual Size.

- ► To see, without printing, how your printout will look after changing Page Setup options, perform the steps on the previous page, but click on Preview rather than on OK in step 6.

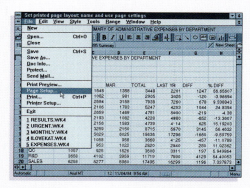

► **1** Open the worksheet file for which you want to make Page Setup changes. Then, click on File in the menu bar and click on the Page Setup command. (If you already have the Print dialog box open, as described on the previous page, you can instead click on the Page Setup button.)

8 When you're done changing Page Setup options, click on the OK button. These options will now be in effect every time you print from this worksheet file (see previous page), or until you change the options again by repeating the steps on this page.

These settings produce the header and footer you see on this page's sample printout.

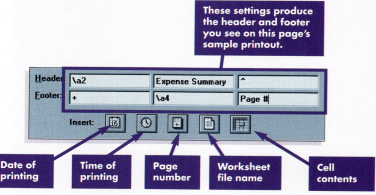

| Header: | \a2 | Expense Summary | ^ |
| Footer: | + | \a4 | Page # |

Insert:

| Date of printing | Time of printing | Page number | Worksheet file name | Cell contents |

7 Next, type the desired text and/or use the buttons below the boxes to insert special codes for printing the date of printing, the time of printing, the page number, the worksheet file name, or the contents of a specific cell. (If you choose to print the contents of a specific cell, be sure to type a cell address after the backslash (\) code that 1-2-3 inserts. For example, \a2 would print the contents of cell A2.

2 You may be able to fit a wide printout on a single page by changing the printout's orientation from Portrait (upright) to Landscape (sideways). Conversely, long printouts generally print better with the Portrait setting.

3 Another way to fit data on one page is to shrink the data. To do this, open the Size drop-down list box and choose Fit all to page.

4 To center your data horizontally (left to right) on the page, check Horizontally. To center your data vertically (top to bottom), check Vertically. To center your data both ways (a popular option), check both.

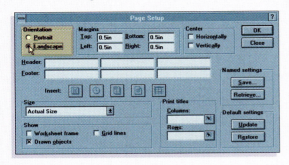

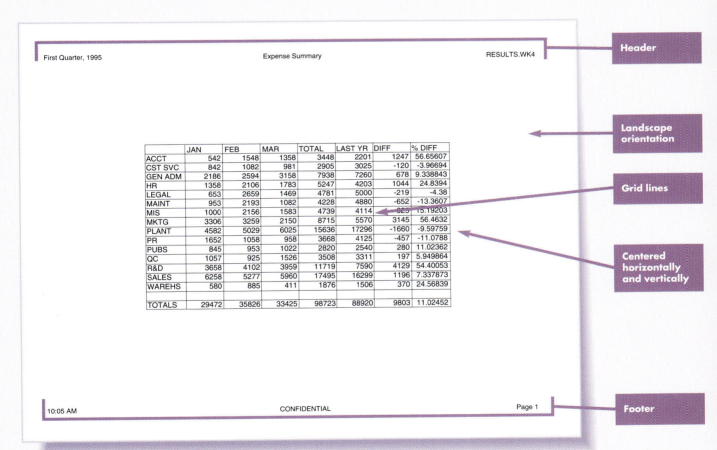

First Quarter, 1995 — Expense Summary — RESULTS.WK4

Header

Landscape orientation

Grid lines

Centered horizontally and vertically

	JAN	FEB	MAR	TOTAL	LAST YR	DIFF	% DIFF
ACCT	542	1548	1358	3448	2201	1247	56.65607
CST SVC	842	1082	981	2905	3025	-120	-3.96694
GEN ADM	2186	2594	3158	7938	7260	678	9.338843
HR	1358	2106	1783	5247	4203	1044	24.8394
LEGAL	653	2659	1469	4781	5000	-219	-4.38
MAINT	953	2193	1082	4228	4880	-652	-13.3607
MIS	1000	2156	1583	4739	4114	625	15.19203
MKTG	3306	3259	2150	8715	5570	3145	56.4632
PLANT	4582	5029	6025	15636	17296	-1660	-9.59759
PR	1652	1058	958	3668	4125	-457	-11.0788
PUBS	845	953	1022	2820	2540	280	11.02362
QC	1057	925	1526	3508	3311	197	5.949864
R&D	3658	4102	3959	11719	7590	4129	54.40053
SALES	6258	5277	5960	17495	16299	1196	7.337873
WAREHS	580	885	411	1876	1506	370	24.56839
TOTALS	29472	35826	33425	98723	88920	9803	11.02452

10:05 AM — CONFIDENTIAL — Page 1

Footer

6 To print descriptive text at the top (header) or bottom (footer) of each printout page, first click in any of the six Header or Footer text boxes. Items you place in the leftmost boxes print at the top left or bottom left of each page, items in the center boxes print at the top center or bottom center of each page, and items in the rightmost boxes print at the top right or bottom right of each page.

5 To print the on-screen grid lines that separate cells, check Grid lines. If you *don't* want to print grid lines, make sure that Grid lines is *not* checked.

TRY IT!

Here's an opportunity to try out the many 1-2-3 skills you've acquired in the first seven chapters of this book. Follow these steps to create the worksheet pictured here. For many steps, we've included chapter numbers to help you find more information on the skills required. In upcoming chapters, you'll learn about certain techniques that would make this sheet more readable. For example, you will learn how to align the column headings over the numbers below them and how to express the % DIFF figures in fewer decimal places.

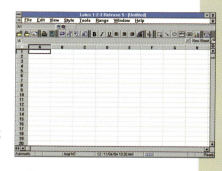

Save and close any open worksheet files that you've been working on. A new, blank worksheet will appear. *Chapter 6*

REVENUES BY CATEGORY, IN THOUSANDS
First Quarter, 1995

	JAN	FEB	MAR	TOTAL	LAST YR	DIFF	% DIFF
CORP							
DIR MAIL	366	410	396	1172	1259	−87	−6.91025
MISC DIR	330	325	215	870	777	93	11.96911
PROMO	58	88	41	187	210	−23	−10.9524
RETAIL	54	154	135	343	320	23	7.1875
	626	527	596	1749	1630	119	7.300613
TOTAL							
	1434	1504	1383	4321	4196	125	2.979028

	A	B	C	D
1	REVENUES BY CATEGORY, IN THOUSANDS			
2	1q, 1995			

Press the Caps Lock key (to make typing in uppercase easier), and in cell A1 type **REVENUES BY CATEGORY, IN THOUSANDS**. *Chapter 4*

Click on the Confirm button to enter the text you just typed. *Chapter 4*

	A	B	C	D
1	REVENUES BY CATEGORY, IN THOUSANDS			
2	1q, 1995			
3				

Click in cell A2 to make it the current cell, press Caps Lock to switch back to normal typing, type **1q, 1995** (short for *First Quarter, 1995*) and press Enter. *Chapter 4*

	A	B	C	D	E	F	G	H
1	REVENUES BY CATEGORY, IN THOUSANDS							
2	1q, 1995							
3								
4		JAN	FEB	MAR	TOTAL	LAST YR	DIFF	% DIFF
5	CORP							
6	DIR MAIL							
7	MISC DIR							
8	PROMO							
9	RETAIL							
10								
11	TOTAL							

Enter all of the remaining column and row headings as shown here. Use the Confirm button, Enter key, or arrow keys as desired to enter each heading. *Chapter 4*

		JAN	FEB	MAR
4		JAN	FEB	MAR
5	CORP	366	410	396
6	DIR MAIL	330	325	215
7	MISC DIR	58	88	41
8	PROMO	54	154	135
9	RETAIL	626	527	596

Enter the January, February, and March data for each of the five categories as shown here. *Chapter 4*

		JAN	FEB	MAR
4		JAN	FEB	MAR
5	CORP	366	410	396
6	DIR MAIL	330	325	215
7	MISC DIR	58	88	41
8	PROMO	54	154	135
9	RETAIL	626	527	596
10				
11	TOTAL	@sum(b5..b9)		
12				

In cell B11, enter **@sum(b5..b9)**. This formula sums the five numbers above cell B11. *Chapter 4*

		JAN	FEB	MAR
4		JAN	FEB	MAR
5	CORP	366	410	396
6	DIR MAIL	330	325	215
7	MISC DIR	58	88	41
8	PROMO	54	154	135
9	RETAIL	626	527	596
10				
11	TOTAL	1434	1504	1383

In cell C11, enter a formula to sum the February data, and in cell D11, enter a formula to sum the March data. (Hint: Use the @SUM function as in step 8 but with different ranges.) *Chapter 4*

In cell E5, enter **@sum(b5..d5)** to add the totals for corporate revenues in row 5. *Chapter 4*

		JAN	FEB	MAR	TOTAL	LAST YR
4		JAN	FEB	MAR	TOTAL	LAST YR
5	CORP	366	410	396	@sum(b5..d5)	
6	DIR MAIL	330	325	215		
7	MISC DIR	58	88	41		
8	PROMO	54	154	135		
9	RETAIL	626	527	596		
10						
11	TOTAL	1434	1504	1383		

Continue to next page ▶

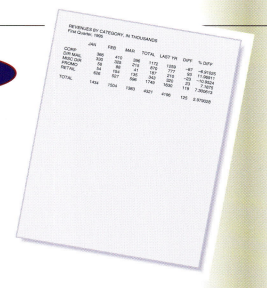

Using the
@SUM func-
tion as in step 9 but with different cell
ranges, fill in the rest of the TOTAL column.
For example, in cell E6 enter **@sum(b6..d6)**.
In cell E11, enter **@sum(b11..d11)** to get a
grand total by summing the sums calculated
in row 11. *Chapter 4*

Enter the
data as
shown for
the LAST YR
column.
These num-
bers (includ-
ing the total
in cell F11)
are plain data, not formula results.
Chapter 4

In cell G5,
enter the for-
mula **+e5-f5**
to subtract
last year's first-quarter revenues from
this year's. Then, in cells G6 through
G9 and cell G11, enter similar formulas, adjusting only the cell references.
For example, the formula in cell G6
should be **+E6-F6**. *Chapter 4*

In cell H5,
enter the for-
mula **+g5/f5**
and observe
the result: –0.0691. This formula expresses the
difference between last year's quarterly revenues
in the Corporate category and this year's as a
proportion of last year's quarterly Corporate
revenues. You need to multiply this number by
100 to get a percentage figure. *Chapter 4*

Double-click
cell H5 to
enter Edit mode. If necessary, place the
insertion point at the end of the formula. *Chapter 5*

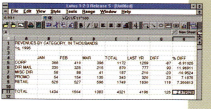

Type ***100**
and enter
your edited
formula.
Notice that cell H5 now shows the correct percentage figure: -6.91025.
Chapter 5

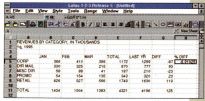

Enter similar
formulas,
with appro-
priate cell
references, in
cells H6 through H9 and cell H11.
Chapter 4

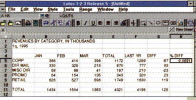

Move to cell A2, type **First Quarter,
1995** and press Enter to replace this
cell's contents. *Chapter 5*

18

Click on File in the menu bar and then click on the Save command. *Chapter 6*

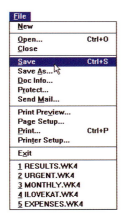

19

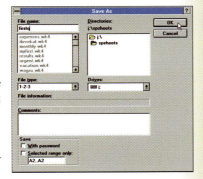

Type **firstq** in the File name text box of the Save As dialog box. Then click on the OK button to save the worksheet file under the name FIRSTQ.WK4. *Chapter 6*

20

Double-click on the A worksheet tab. *Chapter 6*

21

Type **First Quarter** to identify the sheet as containing first-quarter data. Then press Enter. *Chapter 6*

22

Click on File in the menu bar and then click on the Print command. *Chapter 7*

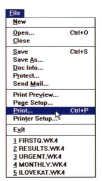

23

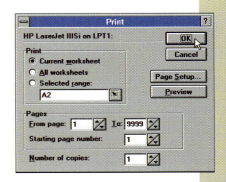

In the Print dialog box, verify that Current worksheet is marked, and then click on the OK button to print one copy of the worksheet. *Chapter 7*

24

Click on File in the menu bar and then click on the Save command to update your worksheet file on disk. *Chapter 6*

25

Click on File in the menu bar and then click on the Close command to close the worksheet file. *Chapter 6*

CHAPTER 8

Changing Worksheet Structure

As your business evolves, so do your 1-2-3 worksheets. What happens to your personnel worksheets when employees come and go? What about when the accounting department tells you that the numbers you budgeted to one category belong under another?

Changes like these require more than the cell-editing techniques you learned in Chapter 5. They require you to restructure your worksheets. Worksheet restructuring was a major headache in the days of ledger books. With 1-2-3, though, it's a breeze.

This chapter covers the most important types of worksheet restructuring. You'll learn how to accommodate new data by adding columns and rows to a sheet. You'll learn how to delete cells and cell contents—including entire columns and rows. You'll discover how to move and copy data from one part of a worksheet file to another by *dragging and dropping*. And you'll see how to adjust the width of a column so that it displays all the data inside it without wasting space.

How to Insert Columns and Rows

To add new data to a worksheet, you have to make room for it. As an example, let's say you have a personnel sheet whose rows are arranged in alphabetical order by the employee's last name. When a new employee joins the company, you must add this person not at the bottom of the sheet but in the proper alphabetical location. One way to do this is to add a blank row to the sheet and then insert the new data. Let's see how.

TIP SHEET

▶ There's an alternative to adding rows of data in certain places just to maintain alphabetical order or another sequencing scheme. Instead, add the rows anywhere—maybe below all the existing rows—and later sort the data using 1-2-3's powerful Sort command. (See Chapter 14.)

▶ When you insert columns or rows, data below or to the right of the new columns or rows shifts. What happens to formulas containing references to the shifted data? 1-2-3 corrects them automatically. For example, in step 5 you can see that Doris Tashjian's vacation data, formerly in row 6, is now in row 7. Cell H6 used to contain @SUM(D6..G6). Now that Tashjian's data has shifted down, her vacation balance, now in cell H7, is calculated with the formula @SUM(D7..G7).

▶ Data you add within the range of an existing formula are calculated in that formula. For example, if your worksheet contains the formula @SUM(D4..D8) and you add a row of data above row 6, the data in the new row will become part of the calculation. The formula will now read @SUM(D4..D9). However, data added outside the range of a formula are not calculated in that formula—a situation that you may need to remedy. Using the same example, if you add a new row below row 8 and you want the new data to be part of the formula, you must manually edit it to read @SUM(D4..D9).

Insert two columns to the left of column G.

1 If you want to insert a single column, move to any cell in the column immediately to the right of where you want to insert the new one. To insert multiple columns, indicate the number of columns to insert by selecting at least one cell in the same number of columns, starting in the column immediately to the right of where you want to insert the new ones. For example, to insert two columns to the left of column G, select at least one cell in each of columns G and H. Then skip to step 3.

New row

5 Your new column(s) or row(s) are inserted. Add data to these columns or rows as you normally would.

Insert one row above row 4.

2 If you want instead to insert a single row, move to any cell in the row immediately below where you want to insert the new one. To insert multiple rows, indicate the number of rows to insert by selecting at least one cell in the same number of rows, starting in the row immediately below where you want to insert the new ones. For example, to insert three rows above row 4, select at least one cell in each of rows 4, 5, and 6.

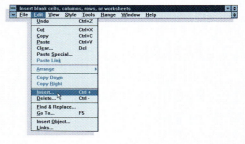

3 Click on Edit in the menu bar and then click on the Insert command.

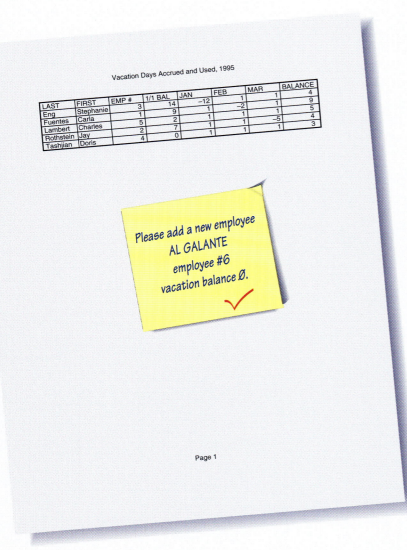

Vacation Days Accrued and Used, 1995

LAST	FIRST	EMP #	1/1 BAL	JAN	FEB	MAR	BALANCE
							4
Eng	Stephanie	3	14	−12	1	1	9
Fuentes	Carla	1	9	1	−2	1	5
Lambert	Charles	5	2	1	1	−5	4
Rothstein	Jay	2	7	1	1	1	3
Tashjian	Doris	4	0	1	1		

Please add a new employee AL GALANTE employee #6 vacation balance Ø. ✓

4 In the Insert dialog box, click on the appropriate radio button, Column or Row, and then click on OK.

How to Delete or Clear Cells

To *delete* a cell is to remove the cell from the worksheet, closing up the vacated space by shifting either the cells on the right or the cells below. To *clear* a cell is to delete its contents and leave the cell empty. Often, you delete an entire row or column. For example, in a personnel worksheet, you might delete the row containing the data of an employee who left the company. On the other hand, you may need to clear any number of cells—even nonadjacent ones—when you know the data they contain are wrong or outdated but you do not yet know what to put in their place.

▶ **1** If you want to *delete* cells, continue on to step 2. If you want instead to *clear* cells, skip to step 6.

7 Press the Delete key.

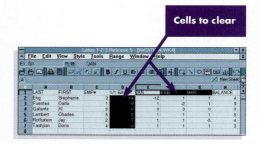

Cells to clear

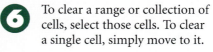

6 To clear a range or collection of cells, select those cells. To clear a single cell, simply move to it.

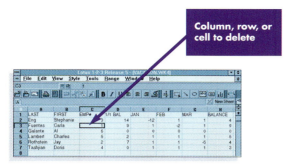

Column, row, or cell to delete

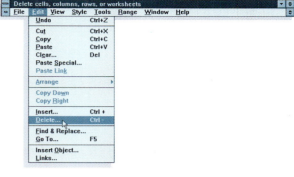

2 To delete a single cell, first move to that cell. To delete an entire column or row, first move to any cell in the column or row. To delete multiple adjacent columns or rows, first select at least one cell in each one. To delete a specific range of cells (collections are not allowed here) rather than entire columns or rows, first select that range.

3 Click on Edit in the menu bar and then click on the Delete command.

Vacation Days Accrued and Used, 1995

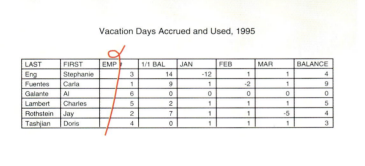

LAST	FIRST	EMP #	1/1 BAL	JAN	FEB	MAR	BALANCE
Eng	Stephanie	3	14	-12	1	1	4
Fuentes	Carla	1	9	1	-2	1	9
Galante	Al	6	0	0	0	0	0
Lambert	Charles	5	2	1	1	1	5
Rothstein	Jay	2	7	1	1	-5	4
Tashjian	Doris	4	0	1	1	1	3

4 In the Delete dialog box, mark the appropriate radio button or check box: Column, Row, or Delete selection. If you mark Delete selection, use the Column and Row radio buttons to control which cells—those to the right of or those below the selection—will shift. If Column is marked, cells to the right will shift left; if Row is marked, cells below will shift up.

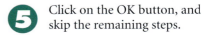

5 Click on the OK button, and skip the remaining steps.

How to Move and Copy Data

1-2-3's "drag-and-drop" editing feature is one of the most intuitive operations in all of computerdom. It enables you to move or copy data by dragging it into place with the mouse much as you might scoop something up and reposition it with your bare hands.

Range to move or copy

▶ **1** Move to the cell or select the range of cells you want to move or copy. (You cannot drag-and-drop collections.)

▶ Before dragging cells, make sure there's room for them in their intended location. If necessary, insert new columns and/or rows. (See "How to Insert Columns and Rows" earlier in this chapter.)

▶ When you move cells (step 5), the vacated cells are cleared, not deleted. Thus, empty cells remain on your worksheet. See the preceding page if you want to delete these empty cells.

▶ When you move cells, formulas that reference those cells individually update to reflect the new cell location; thus, formula results remain accurate. Likewise, if you move entire referenced ranges, formulas update accordingly. However, if you move cells that are only *part* of a referenced range, 1-2-3 can become confused about which cells should and should not be part of the referenced range, and formulas may display erroneous results. Whenever possible, move entire referenced ranges at a time. After moving data in any case, carefully check formulas that reference ranges, and edit those formulas as necessary.

7 If you drop the cell(s) onto cells already containing data, 1-2-3 asks you whether you want to replace the data in those cells with the data you're dropping. If you do, click on the OK button; otherwise, click on the Cancel button to cancel the operation altogether, and then start again at step 1.

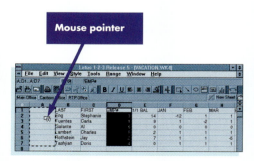

Mouse pointer

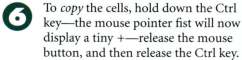

6 To *copy* the cells, hold down the Ctrl key—the mouse pointer fist will now display a tiny +—release the mouse button, and then release the Ctrl key.

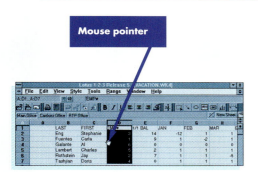

Mouse pointer

2 Point to the border of the cell or range (avoid the lower-right corner) so that the mouse pointer changes to an open hand.

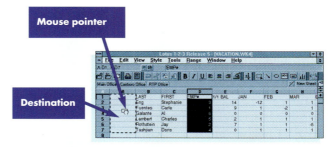

Mouse pointer

Destination

3 Hold down the left mouse button and drag to the desired location. As you drag, the mouse pointer changes to a fist grabbing a rectangle. Also, a dotted outline indicates where the cell(s) you are moving or copying will be dropped if you release the mouse button at that moment.

Vacation Days Accrued and Used, 1995

EMP #	LAST	FIRST	EMP #	1/1 BAL	JAN	FEB	MAR	BALANCE
3	Eng	Stephanie	3	14	-12	1	1	4
1	Fuentes	Carla	1	9	1	-2	1	9
6	Galante	Al	6	0	0	0	0	0
5	Lambert	Charles	5	2	1	1	1	5
2	Rothstein	Jay	2	7	1	1	-5	4
4	Tashjian	Doris	4	0	1	1	1	3

DRAG & DROP

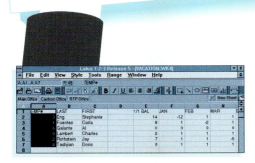

5 To *move* the cell(s), simply release the mouse button.

4 To drag the data to a portion of the worksheet that's not currently visible, drag to the appropriate edge of the worksheet. 1-2-3 will scroll the sheet automatically. To drag to another sheet in the same worksheet file, drag to the desired sheet's worksheet tab and then down onto that sheet. Or, drag to the New Sheet button to both create and drag to a new worksheet.

How to Adjust Column Width

1-2-3's default column width is often inadequate to display long headings, large numbers, and numbers taken to many decimal places. When a column is not wide enough to display its contents, 1-2-3 truncates it, expresses it in scientific notation, or simply displays asterisks (***). However, 1-2-3 always "remembers" the complete contents of the cell, displaying it in the contents box when the cell is current, and using it whenever the cell is referenced in a formula. To display the complete contents in the cell, you can widen the column. Through the same technique, you can narrow a space-wasting column so that it's no wider than necessary.

Mouse pointer

▶ **1** To adjust the width of a single column, point to the right edge of that column's column letter so that the mouse pointer changes to a vertical bar with arrows emerging from each side.

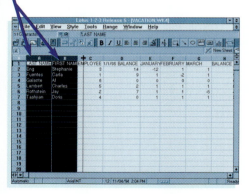

Both columns will be resized equally.

5 To adjust the width of multiple columns at one time, drag across the desired column letters to select adjacent columns, or hold down the Ctrl key as you click on column letters to select nonadjacent columns. Then, follow steps 1 though 3, dragging from the right edge of any column letter in the selection. Each selected column will have the exact same width.

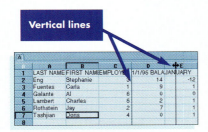

Vertical lines

2 Hold down the left mouse button and drag to the right (to widen the column) or to the left (to narrow it). As you drag, dark vertical lines indicate the column's new width should you release the mouse button at that moment.

3 Release the mouse button and observe the data within the column to determine whether the column has reached its optimal width. Are data truncated unnecessarily? Or, on the other hand, is space wasted?

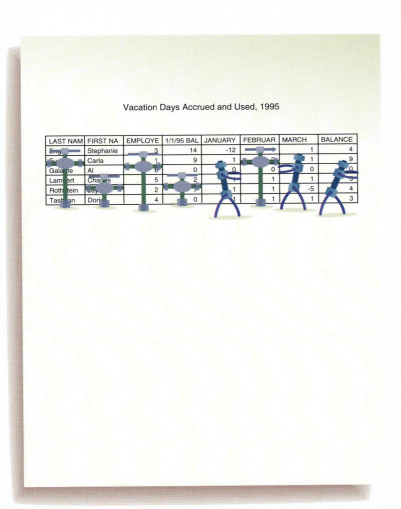

Vacation Days Accrued and Used, 1995

4 Repeat steps 1 through 3 to further refine the column width and to adjust other columns.

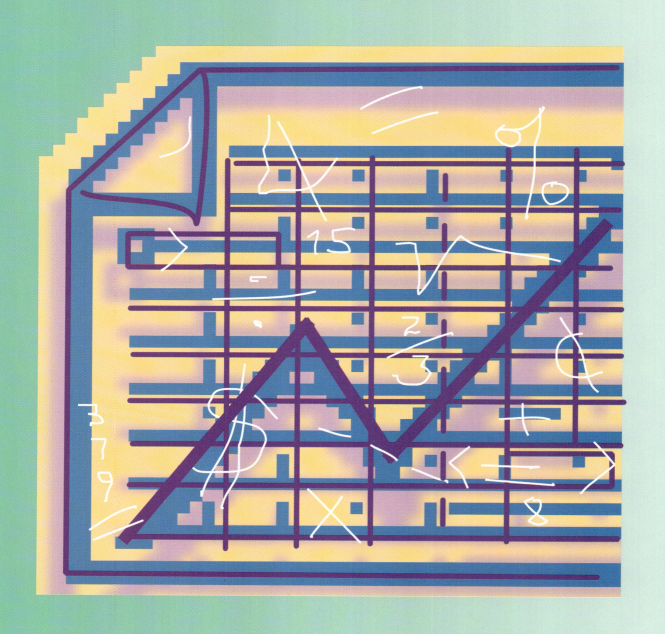

CHAPTER 9

Improving Worksheet Appearance

You build a worksheet mainly for accuracy and usability, but there's room for aesthetics, too. Cell-content enhancements such as boldface or italics can draw the eyes toward important information. Rounding numbers off to a reasonable number of decimal places can help you and your readers put data in perspective. And a nice-looking worksheet generally garners more attention—an important part of any effective communications effort.

1-2-3 offers a variety of formatting, or *style*, features that can improve the appearance of your worksheets both on the screen and in print. In this chapter, you will learn how to format cell contents and numbers, how to enhance cells by applying special backgrounds and borders, how to change the alignment of cell contents within cells, and how to align long headings across multiple cells.

1-2-3 makes it pretty easy to apply sophisticated formatting to your worksheets. Don't let this ease tempt you into excessive formatting. An overly formatted worksheet wastes your time, masks information, and impresses no one. Apply formatting judiciously and you'll find it far more effective.

How to Format Cell Contents

Cell-content formatting enables you to change the appearance of characters within cells. Formatting choices for cell-content formatting include typeface (such as Arial and Times New Roman), text attributes (such as boldface and italics), and size (measured by height in points, where 72 points equal 1 inch). To format cell contents in 1-2-3, you actually format the cell. Whatever happens to be in the cell takes on the assigned format, and the formatting remains in effect even if you change the cell contents. You can format a cell even when it's blank; later, when you enter cell contents, those contents take on the assigned formatting.

TIP SHEET

► As you change settings in the Font & Attributes dialog box, keep an eye on the Sample box. It shows you how your cell contents will look if you OK the dialog box at that moment.

► The typefaces available in the Face list (step 3) will vary depending on your printer and Windows setups. In addition, the available type sizes and text attributes can vary depending on what typeface you've selected.

► To reverse the effects of a formatting change, simply repeat the steps shown here, making selections matching the original formatting. Or, select the cell(s), click on Edit in the menu bar, click on the Clear command, click on Styles only, and then click on OK. This second procedure will restore not only cell-content formatting, but also will remove every other type of formatting described in this chapter.

► After formatting cells, you may have to adjust column widths to accommodate the now wider or narrower cell contents.

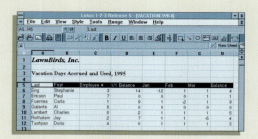

1 Move to the cell you want to format, or select a range or collection of cells to format them all.

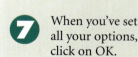

7 When you've set all your options, click on OK.

6 To change the color of cell contents, use the Color drop-down list to select a new color. If you don't have a color printer, all colors except pure white will print as black, but color can still be useful for on-screen purposes.

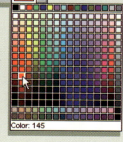

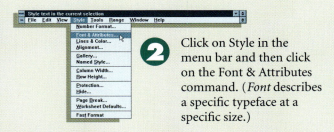

② Click on Style in the menu bar and then click on the Font & Attributes command. (*Font* describes a specific typeface at a specific size.)

③ To change the typeface, scroll the Face list as necessary, and then click on the desired typeface's name.

LawnBirds, Inc.

Vacation Days Accrued and Used, 1995

Last	First	Employee #	1/1 Balance	Jan	Feb	Mar	Balance
Eng	Stephanie	3	14	-12	1	1	4
Ericson	Paul	8	0	0	0	1	1
Fuentes	Carla	1	9	1	-2	1	9
Galante	Al	6	0	0	0	0	0
Lambert	Charles	5	2	1	1	1	5
Rothstein	Jay	2	7	1	1	-5	4
Tashjian	Doris	4	0	1	1	1	3

④ To change the type size, scroll the Size list as necessary, and then click on the desired size. (Remember, size is measured by height in points; 12 points equals ⅙ inch, 24 points equals ⅓ inch.)

⑤ To change text attributes, check or uncheck Attributes options as desired. (Checking Normal automatically unchecks every other Attributes option.) Use the Underline drop-down list as desired to select any one of three underline styles.

How to Format Numbers

1-2-3 usually uses its Automatic number format for the display of numbers in worksheet cells. Elements of this format include displaying minus signs to denote negative numbers and leaving out the commas that commonly separate thousands. However, you can choose from a wide array of other number formats. For example, you can format a cell containing a dollar amount to include a dollar sign, to express no decimal places (rounding numbers to the nearest dollar), and to display negative numbers in parentheses. Number formatting affects only the display of numbers within worksheet cells. The complete number or formula appears in the contents box when the cell is current, and the complete number is always used in calculations.

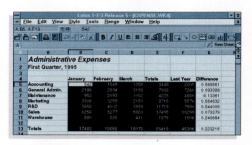

▶ **1** Move to the cell whose number format you want to change, or select a range or collection of cells to format them all.

2 Click on Style in the menu bar and then click on the Number Format command.

3 Scroll the Format list as necessary, and then click on the format name that best describes the type of number you have entered or plan to enter in the current or selected cells.

4 When you select certain number formats, additional formatting options appear. For example, when you select Currency, you also have the option of setting the number of decimal places and which currency symbol to use (for example, $ for U.S. Dollars or ¥ for Japanese Yen). Set these options as desired.

5 If you'd like to enclose your numbers in parentheses, check Parens. Because the Currency and Comma formats automatically enclose *negative* numbers in parentheses, negative numbers with these formats will now display with *double* parentheses.

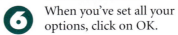

6 When you've set all your options, click on OK.

How to Format Cell Backgrounds and Borders

By default, worksheet cells have plain white backgrounds and nonprinting borders. Formatting cell backgrounds and borders, however, are excellent ways to highlight important worksheet information and to improve general worksheet appearance, both on screen and in print. Like all formatting, backgrounds and borders should be applied sparingly lest they lose their impact or overly clutter your worksheet. Common uses of backgrounds include shading column headings and adding a thick border to a cell that contains a grand total. When working with ranges, you have the choice of placing a border around entire ranges or along every edge of each selected cell.

TIP SHEET

▶ Unlike cell grid lines, which print only if you specify them in the Page Setup dialog box (see Chapter 7), cell backgrounds and borders always print.

▶ More than any other type of cell formatting, the wrong backgrounds and borders can create very unreadable and very ugly printouts. To remove backgrounds and borders, use the Edit menu's Clear command as described earlier in this chapter under "How to Format Cell Contents."

▶ After formatting backgrounds and borders, your selected cells may appear very different than what you expected. Deselect the cells, and things should look much better.

▶ Printing colored cells on a noncolor printer can be a tricky matter. Colored backgrounds and borders may print in black, white, or shades of gray, while text prints only in black or white. To get an idea, without printing, of how your printout will look, preview your worksheet as described in Chapter 7.

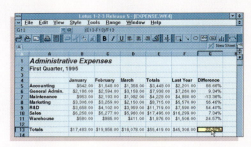

1 Move to the cell you want to format, or select a range or collection of cells to format them all.

8 Take one last look at the Sample box to make sure that you aren't about to create a formatting monstrosity. If all is well, click on the OK button.

7 For an extra touch of class, you can add a *designer frame*—that is, a fancy outline— around the current cell or selected range(s). To do so, choose the desired frame style from the Designer frame drop-down list (when you do, 1-2-3 automatically checks Designer frame for you) and optionally choose a frame color from the Frame color drop-down list.

② Click on Style in the menu bar and then click on the Lines & Color command.

③ To change cell backgrounds, use the Background color, Pattern, and/or Pattern color drop-down lists to create the desired background. Use the Sample box as a guide.

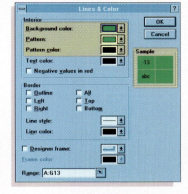

④ If the text in the Sample box is now difficult to read, use the Text color drop-down list to select a more readable color. (This drop-down list has a direct connection to the Font & Attributes dialog box's Color drop-down list covered earlier in this chapter.) Note that unless you have a color printer, all text colors except pure white will print as black, regardless of what the Sample box shows.

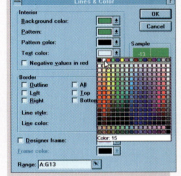

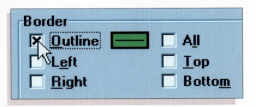

⑤ To place a border around the current cell, selected range, or each range in a collection, check Outline. To place a border along just certain edges of the current or selected cells, click on the appropriate option(s): Left, Right, Top, and/or Bottom. To place a border along every edge of every selected cell, check All, which automatically checks every other option for you.

⑥ To customize the line style and color of your borders, use the Line style and/or Line color drop-down lists.

How to Align Cell Contents

B y default, 1-2-3 right-aligns numbers, including formula results, within each cell, and left-aligns text. Sometimes, though, this alignment scheme is inadequate. It's especially problematic when left-aligned column headings (text) are atop columns of right-aligned numbers. However, 1-2-3 makes it easy to change the way cell contents align within cells. As with the other formatting covered in this chapter, when you change alignment, you technically are formatting the cell, not the cell contents. Therefore, if you later change the cell contents, the alignment you set remains in effect.

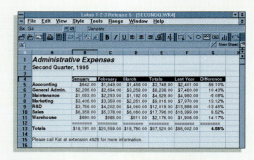

1 Move to the cell whose alignment you want to change, or select a range or collection of cells to format them all.

TIP SHEET

▸ **To return selected cells to their original alignment, repeat the steps here, resetting each option as required. Or, use the Edit menu's Clear command as described earlier in this chapter under "How to Format Cell Contents."**

▸ **Sometimes numbers are used not for calculations but as *labels*—identifying data such as column and row headings. For example, in a worksheet comparing yearly results, each of several years (1994, 1995, 1996,...) might be a column heading. However, 1-2-3 will right-align these numbers unless you specifically indicate that the numbers are labels. To do this, type an apostrophe (') before the number. (You may have noticed that 1-2-3 inserts an apostrophe automatically when you enter text or mixed text and numbers.) For example, enter '1995 to display 1995 as a label. As you saw in step 5, the apostrophe also is useful for identifying special characters (such as = + @) as labels rather than as formula components.**

▸ **You cannot decimally align numbers using the procedure described on this page. Instead, apply to the cells containing those numbers any number format that allows you to set decimal places.**

7 When you've set all your alignment options, click on OK.

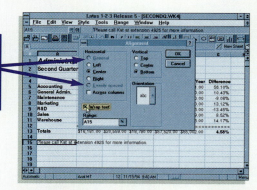

These options cannot be used in conjunction with Wrap text.

6 To cause wide cell contents to break into separate lines within a cell rather than being truncated or spilling into adjacent cells, check Wrap text. 1-2-3 will automatically increase row height to accommodate multiple-line cell contents.

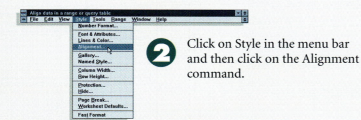

2 Click on Style in the menu bar and then click on the Alignment command.

3 Under Horizontal in the Alignment dialog box, click on the radio button for the alignment you want, as described in the next two steps. (The Across columns option is described on the next page.)

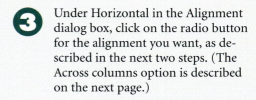

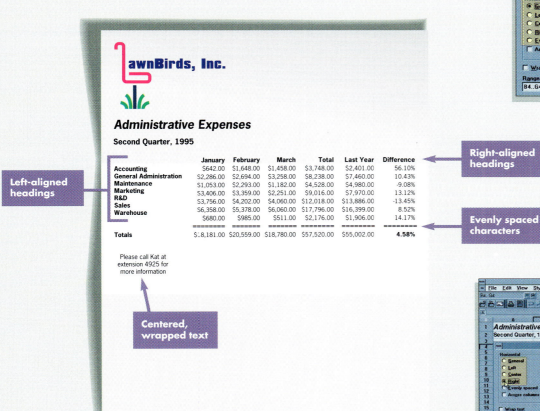

Left-aligned headings

Right-aligned headings

Evenly spaced characters

Centered, wrapped text

LawnBirds, Inc.

Administrative Expenses

Second Quarter, 1995

	January	February	March	Total	Last Year	Difference
Accounting	$642.00	$1,648.00	$1,458.00	$3,748.00	$2,401.00	56.10%
General Administration	$2,286.00	$2,694.00	$3,258.00	$8,238.00	$7,460.00	10.43%
Maintenance	$1,053.00	$2,293.00	$1,182.00	$4,528.00	$4,980.00	-9.08%
Marketing	$3,406.00	$3,359.00	$2,251.00	$9,016.00	$7,970.00	13.12%
R&D	$3,756.00	$4,202.00	$4,060.00	$12,018.00	$13,886.00	-13.45%
Sales	$6,358.00	$5,378.00	$6,060.00	$17,796.00	$16,399.00	8.52%
Warehouse	$680.00	$985.00	$511.00	$2,176.00	$1,906.00	14.17%
Totals	$18,181.00	$20,559.00	$18,780.00	$57,520.00	$55,002.00	4.58%

Please call Kat at extension 4925 for more information

4 The default General option aligns text to the left and numbers to the right. Left aligns all data to the left. Center centers data between a cell's left and right edges. Right aligns all data to the right.

5 The Evenly spaced option in most cases adds space between each character in a cell to make the contents stretch from the cell's left to right edge. (To enter the multiple equal signs shown here, be sure to precede them with an apostrophe in each cell. Otherwise, 1-2-3 will refuse to let you enter the cell contents.)

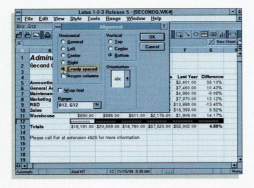

How to Align Cell Contents over Multiple Columns

A major heading in a worksheet may look better when centered or evenly spaced over the entire worksheet or over the columns to which it refers. 1-2-3 helps you achieve this effect in just a few steps.

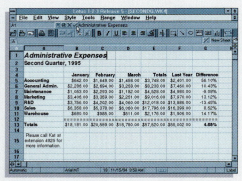

1 Enter the heading in column A or in the leftmost column of the group over which the heading is to be aligned.

2 Select the heading and, to its right, all the cells in columns over which the heading will be centered.

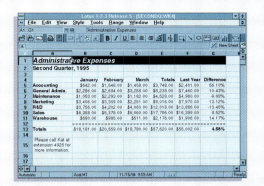

3 Click on Style in the menu bar and then click on the Alignment command.

Evenly spaced across multiple columns

Centered across multiple columns

4 Under Horizontal, click on the radio button for the type of alignment you want. For example, to stretch text over the selected cells, click on Evenly spaced.

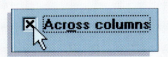

5 Check Across columns.

6 Click on OK.

CHAPTER 10

Adding Worksheet Capabilities

1-2-3 comes with a vast array of tools designed to make your worksheets easier to build and more functional. Some of these tools are so specialized that you might use 1-2-3 day in and day out for years and never need them. Yet for other people, these same tools are indispensable. Such is life.

This chapter covers a few tools that *no* 1-2-3 user should be without. You'll learn more about 1-2-3's @functions, which perform operations that would be inconvenient or impossible to perform with ordinary, handmade formulas. You'll learn a great way to build worksheets faster by using "drag and fill" to fill in repetitive formulas—letting 1-2-3 automatically figure out the correct cell references for you! This technique spares you from manually typing similar formulas over and over (and over). And you'll even learn how to override 1-2-3's automatic adjustment of cell references when necessary.

How to Use 1-2-3's @Functions

Chapter 4 explained that *@functions* are time- and effort-saving formulas built into 1-2-3. Some @functions, such as @SUM, are mere conveniences, saving you the trouble of typing long lists of cell references. Other @functions, though, perform calculations that you just couldn't build in a formula yourself. For example, how would you calculate the smallest number in a range? 1-2-3's over 200 built-in @functions enable you to calculate just about anything from simple averages to the cumulative interest portion of a periodic payment! Because of their general usefulness and similarity of use, this page shows you specifically how to use the @AVG, @MAX, and @MIN @functions.

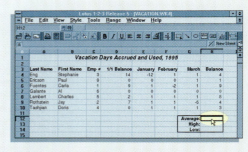

1 Move to the cell where you want to insert the @function formula.

TIP SHEET

▶ If you'd prefer, you can always type an @func-tion manually as you learned in Chapter 4. Using the @function selector, however, saves you the trouble of memorizing @function names, and helps you avoid common typing mistakes like leaving out the @ sign or the parentheses.

▶ Not every @function works by simply defining a range as shown here. To learn more about how to use a specific @function, open the @Function List dialog box shown in step 4, click on the de-sired @function, and then click on the ? button in the dialog box's top-right corner. (You'll learn more about this button in Chapter 11.)

▶ You can use the @functions shown here with col-lections as well. Simply separate the range or cell references with commas—for example, @min(b4..d8,f4..g8,i10,j10).

▶ By convention, @function names are written in uppercase, but when typing them in 1-2-3, you can use uppercase, lowercase, or a combination of the two.

7 Once you've defined the range, enter the completed formula by clicking on the Confirm button or pressing Enter.

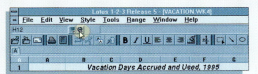

2 Click on the edit line's *@function selector*. (It displays an @ sign and a tiny, down-pointing triangle.)

3 To calculate an average of numbers in a range, click on AVG and then skip to step 6. Otherwise, click on List All.

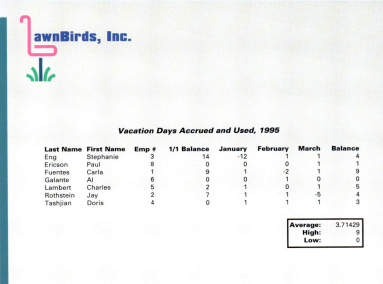

4 The @Functions box lists 1-2-3's over 200 @functions in alphabetical order. Patiently scroll through the list, and then click on MAX to find the largest number in a range, or on MIN to find the smallest such number.

5 Click on OK.

6 1-2-3 inserts most of your @function formula for you, and selects the portion you need to define: the range. You can either manually type the range reference as described in Chapter 4, or simply select the range as described in Chapter 5 to have 1-2-3 fill in the appropriate reference for you.

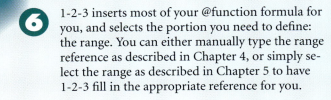

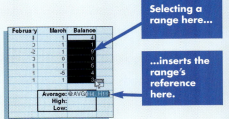

Selecting a range here...

...inserts the range's reference here.

How to "Drag-and-Fill" Formulas

Many worksheets contain sequences of very similar formulas. For example, the right-most column in a table is often a sequence of @SUM formulas that calculate the totals of numbers to their left; the only difference from one formula to the next is the row number. When building a worksheet, you could enter every formula in such a sequence one at a time. But wait! There's a much easier way: It's called "drag-and-fill." When you drag-and-fill to create a sequence of formulas, 1-2-3 automatically—almost magically—adjusts the cell references in the manner it assumes you want it to. Amazingly, it's usually correct.

TIP SHEET

▶ After filling in formulas, check to make sure 1-2-3 adjusted cell references the way you needed. While it is clever, automatic reference adjustment is not infallible. It merely shifts cell references according to the length and direction of the fill. For example, as you fill cells to the right, every column letter in the formula increases by one. Occasionally you may have to override automatic reference adjustment. The next page explains why and how.

▶ Drag-and-fill can also be handy for filling in sequential text and numbers. For example, if you enter *January* in cell A1 and then drag-and-fill cells B1 through G1, 1-2-3 will fill in every month name through *July*. This technique works for many linear progressions, including numbers, years, quarters, dates, and days of the week.

▶ When you drag-and-fill over cells that already contain data, 1-2-3 will replace that data without warning.

▶ When you drag-and-fill, 1-2-3 also carries along any cell formatting (see Chapter 9) from the first cell.

▶ **1** Enter the topmost or leftmost formula in the sequence.

Adjusted cell references

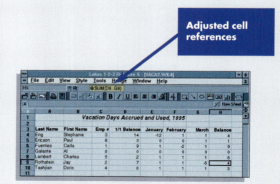

5 Observe what has happened. In the filled-in cells, you now see the formula results. Move to any one of these cells, and the contents box will show you the formula that 1-2-3 has inserted for you. Notice how 1-2-3 has adjusted each formula's cell references accordingly.

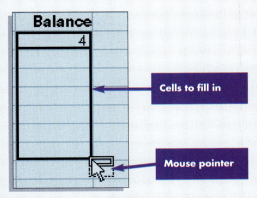

Mouse pointer

2 With the cell containing that formula as the current cell, point to the cell's bottom-right corner until the mouse pointer changes to the shape shown here.

Balance

Cells to fill in

Mouse pointer

3 Drag down or to the right to select the cells you want to fill in. As soon as you start to drag, the mouse pointer assumes the shape shown here.

Balance
| 4 |
| 1 |
| 9 |
| 0 |
| 5 |
| 4 |
| 3 |

4 Release the mouse button to fill in the selected cells.

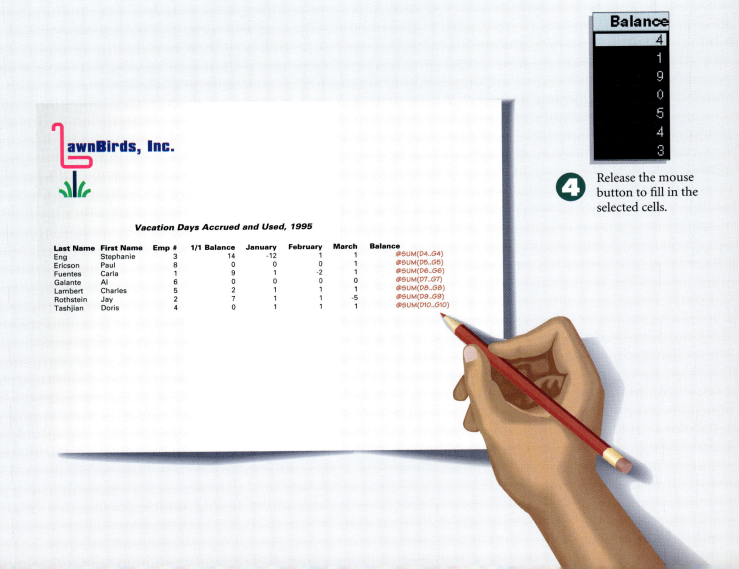

LawnBirds, Inc.

Vacation Days Accrued and Used, 1995

Last Name	First Name	Emp #	1/1 Balance	January	February	March	Balance
Eng	Stephanie	3	14	-12	1	1	@SUM(D4..G4)
Ericson	Paul	8	0	0	0	1	@SUM(D5..G5)
Fuentes	Carla	1	9	1	-2	1	@SUM(D6..G6)
Galante	Al	6	0	0	0	0	@SUM(D7..G7)
Lambert	Charles	5	2	1	1	1	@SUM(D8..G8)
Rothstein	Jay	2	7	1	1	-5	@SUM(D9..G9)
Tashjian	Doris	4	0	1	1	1	@SUM(D10..G10)

How to Work with Absolute References

Look at the sample worksheet on this page. Every number in the Bonus column represents a person's base pay multiplied by 7%, the multiplier in cell B12. You could enter Ms. Eng's bonus (in cell E4) as +D4*B12. But what happens if you try to drag-and-fill the Bonus column as described on the preceding page? The reference to cell D4 increases automatically to D5, D6, and so on, just as you want. But the reference to the multiplier in cell B12 also increases to B13, B14, and so on, producing incorrect results. You need the reference to cell B12 to remain constant. To accomplish this, calculate Ms. Eng's bonus using an *absolute reference* to cell B12. Then, whenever the formula is used in a fill operation, the reference will remain the same.

 1 Move to the cell where you want to enter the formula that will contain the absolute reference.

TIP SHEET

▶ Don't worry about moving a cell that is referenced absolutely. The references to the moved cell adjust automatically to reflect the new location—and they remain absolute.

▶ Why, as in the example on this page, would you reference a cell containing a multiplier rather than just including that multiplier as a number in every bonus calculation? Well, what if you needed to decrease each bonus from 7 to 5 percent? Having referenced a cell rather than typing the multiplier in each formula, you need only enter the new multiplier once—in the referenced cell.

▶ To reference a range absolutely, include a dollar sign before each column letter and row number in the range reference. For example, to reference cells A1 through B4 absolutely, type A1..B4.

▶ To reference a cell or range on another worksheet absolutely, also include a dollar sign before the worksheet name or letter. For example, to reference cell A1 on worksheet C absolutely, type $C:$A$1.

2 Begin typing or editing the formula normally.

3 To type the cell reference that is to remain constant in fill operations, precede both the column letter and row number with a dollar sign ($).

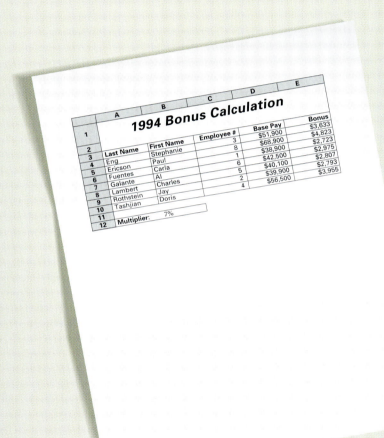

4 Complete and enter the formula normally. The result appears in the cell.

5 Drag-and-fill the formula as described on the previous page.

6 Move to any of the filled-in cells and observe what has happened. The contents box shows you that the normal cell references have adjusted automatically, while the absolute reference remains constant.

CHAPTER 11

Rescue

 Even the best-trained 1-2-3 user makes the occasional error or stumbles into unfamiliar territory. Far be it from Lotus to abandon you in your time of need.

1-2-3's most valuable rescue feature is the Undo command, the first topic of this chapter. The Undo command reverses the last action you performed—entering cell contents, clearing cells, moving data, filling in formulas, and so on. Though it cannot reverse every action, Undo is a good bet to get you out of hot water.

1-2-3 also comes with volumes of online help that you can display on your screen and peruse much as you'd flip through a reference book. Much of 1-2-3's help system is context-sensitive, so it can bring you directly to information on the action in progress. For example, if you issue the Help command when the Print dialog box is displayed, you see information about printing. This chapter explains how to issue the Help command and how to navigate the help system to find more information.

Finally, this chapter covers 1-2-3's spelling checker, which can find and correct misspellings in cells that contain text.

How to Undo an Action

I f it hasn't happened to you yet, it will: You'll edit a formula incorrectly, move some cells when you meant to copy them, drag and drop over important data—and be dismayed or even horrified by the results. Not to worry. If you notice a mistake fast enough, you can probably reverse it instantly by issuing 1-2-3's Undo command. The Undo command can reverse almost every worksheet building, editing, and formatting action. Beware, however, that 1-2-3 cannot undo certain actions, such as saving a worksheet file.

TIP SHEET

▶ Scrolling the worksheet, moving to a different cell or sheet, and selecting a range do not make the previous action irreversible. For example, if you format a cell and then move to another cell (but do nothing else), you can still undo the format.

▶ All settings you make in one session with a dialog box constitute one action and thus can be reversed. Let's say you open the Font & Attributes dialog box and assign a new typeface, size, and color (see Chapter 9). The Undo command will reverse all these changes, not just the last one you selected.

▶ If you've saved your worksheet file recently, you may be able to use another disaster-recovery plan: Close your worksheet file without saving changes, and then reopen the file. Your worksheet file will return to the state it was in when you last issued the Save command. This is another good reason to save your worksheet files frequently.

▶ **1** The Undo command is turned off for some computers. To make sure that Undo is turned on for your computer, first click on Tools in the menu bar and click on the User Setup command.

6 As you can see, the Undo command isn't perfect. Used with care, however, it usually does much more good than harm.

The names have been restored.

5 Observe the results. Did the Undo command work as you had hoped? If so, congratulations! If not, you now have *two* problems: reversing Undo's unwanted reversal and fixing the original problem. (Unfortunately, you can't undo an Undo.)

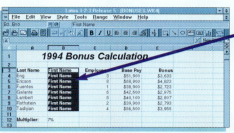

This user accidentally used drag-and-fill to replace every first name.

2 Observe the Undo check box. If it's checked, then Undo is already turned on. Click on Cancel to close the User Setup dialog box without making any changes. If Undo *isn't* checked, however, check it and then click on OK.

3 Once Undo is turned on, 1-2-3 always remembers your last action. As soon as you realize that you want to undo your last action, stop working on your worksheet file. If you perform another action now—even entering one character in a cell—the previous action becomes irreversible.

4 Click on Edit in the menu bar and then click on the Undo command.

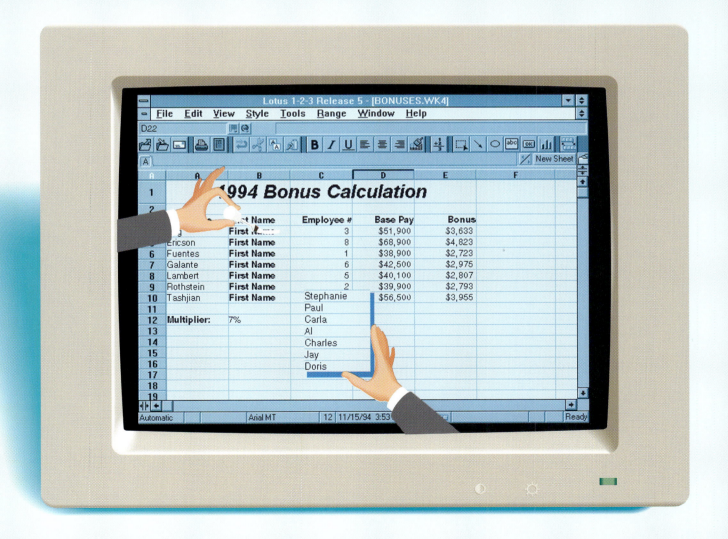

How to Get Online Help

If you have questions as you work with 1-2-3, you can turn to this book for help. But you may well be able to find the information you need without even taking your hands off the keyboard and mouse. 1-2-3's online help system usually gives information related to the action in progress. If it doesn't, you can search through the help system for the information you need. The help system is almost always available, even when a menu is pulled down or a dialog box is displayed.

▶ **1** Press F1 to issue the Help command. If a dialog box is open, you'll see information about that dialog box. If a menu is pulled down, you'll see information about the highlighted command. If you are working in a cell, you'll see information specific to the kind of work you are doing. If nothing else, you'll see a general Help Contents screen.

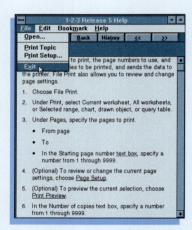

7 The Help window has its own menu bar, separate from 1-2-3's. When you're done using the help system, click on File in the Help window's menu bar and then click on the Exit command.

6 Sometimes you can even click on an icon to jump to a different help screen or to display a definition. If you can, the current help screen will tell you so.

TIP SHEET

▶ You can also get context-sensitive help by clicking on the question-mark (?) icon found in the upper-right corner of dialog boxes.

▶ The Help window is an application window. You can maximize, minimize, restore, resize, and move it. One advantage of this is that you can arrange the Help window so that it does not cover the screen portion you need help with, such as a dialog box. See Chapter 2 for more information on window manipulation.

▶ As you may have noticed already, 1-2-3 automatically displays brief help messages in the title bar whenever you open a menu. Sometimes this is all the help you need.

▶ For *non*–context-sensitive forms of help, explore the commands listed in the Help menu.

2 Read the information displayed in the Help window, using the vertical scroll bar to scroll through it if necessary. (Your Help window may be displayed in a different size and shape than the one shown here.)

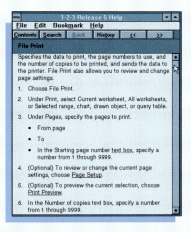

3 To see more information about a solid-underlined topic, click on it. An entirely new help screen appears.

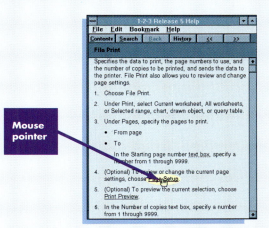

Mouse pointer

Online Help

5 To see the definition of a dotted-underlined topic, click on it. A *definition box* appears. Click anywhere inside this box to close it.

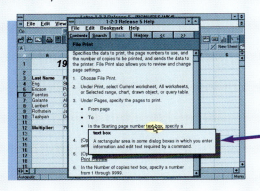

Definition box

4 To go back to the previous help screen, click on the Back button.

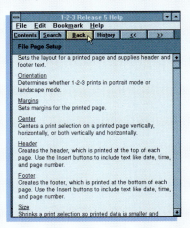

How to Spell-Check a Worksheet File

1-2-3 comes with an electronic dictionary. Upon your command, 1-2-3 checks each word in the current worksheet file against that dictionary. When it comes across a word that's not in the dictionary, 1-2-3 gives you a chance to correct it right away, and even gives you possible corrections from which to choose. Because some correct spellings, such as proper names, unusual words, and foreign-language words, are not in the dictionary, you can tell 1-2-3 to skip over words it does not recognize.

TIP SHEET

▶ **Why not add every correctly spelled word to the dictionary? One reason is that adding words to the dictionary slows down the spelling checker. Don't slow it down with words you hardly ever use. The other reason is that a word can be a valid spelling in one context but not in another. For example, notice in step 4 that *Gough* is not added to the dictionary. That way, 1-2-3 will call attention to it in future spelling checks, where it might be a misspelling for *Cough* or *Gouge*.**

▶ **Besides misspellings, 1-2-3's spelling checker also catches repeated words (such as *the the*) and unusual capitalization (such as *tHe*).**

▶ **1-2-3's dictionary contains many common proper words including first names, last names, cities, states, countries, and geographical features.**

▶ **Beware that the spelling checker won't notice a misspelling that forms another legitimate word, such as misspelling *than* as *then*. Proofread your worksheets carefully to find this type of error.**

 1 If you want to check the spelling of less than the current sheet or entire worksheet file, select the part you want to check. If you want to check a specific sheet, move to that sheet.

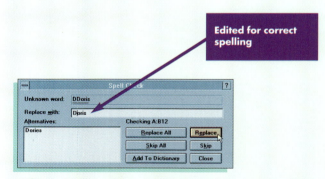

8 Repeat steps 4, 5, 6, or 7 for every unknown word 1-2-3 finds. 1-2-3 tells you when the spelling check is complete; click on OK to close this dialog box.

Edited for correct spelling

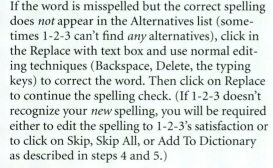

7 If the word is misspelled but the correct spelling does *not* appear in the Alternatives list (sometimes 1-2-3 can't find *any* alternatives), click in the Replace with text box and use normal editing techniques (Backspace, Delete, the typing keys) to correct the word. Then click on Replace to continue the spelling check. (If 1-2-3 doesn't recognize your *new* spelling, you will be required either to edit the spelling to 1-2-3's satisfaction or to click on Skip, Skip All, or Add To Dictionary as described in steps 4 and 5.)

② Click on Tools in the menu bar and then click on the Spell Check command.

③ In the Spell Check dialog box, indicate what part of the worksheet file you want to check: the entire file, the current worksheet, or just the selected range. Then click on OK.

④ When 1-2-3 encounters a word that's not in its dictionary, it displays and underlines that word at the top of the dialog box. If the word is spelled correctly but you don't use it often or it might be a misspelling in another context, click on either Skip or Skip All. Clicking on Skip simply continues the spelling check, ignoring the word in this instance. Clicking on Skip All ignores the word wherever it appears for the rest of this spelling check.

"Gough" is spelled correctly.

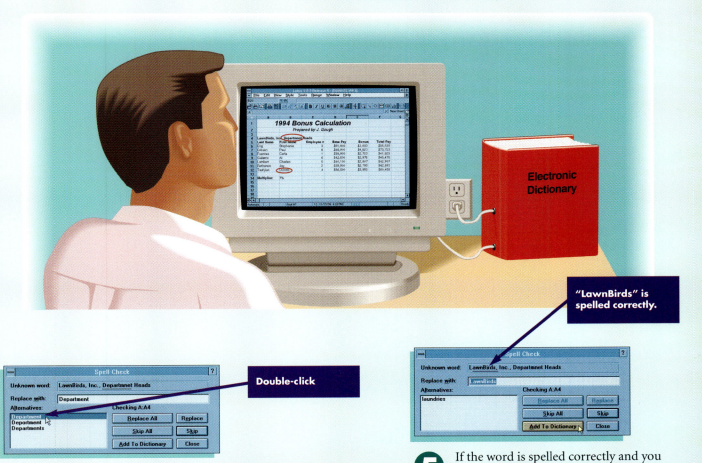

Electronic Dictionary

"LawnBirds" is spelled correctly.

Double-click

⑥ If the word is misspelled and you see the correct spelling in the Alternatives list, double-click on that spelling to correct the word and continue the spelling check.

⑤ If the word is spelled correctly and you plan to use it frequently in other worksheet files, click on Add To Dictionary. This adds the word to 1-2-3's electronic dictionary and continues the spelling check.

TRY IT!

You've built up quite a set of 1-2-3 skills in the last four chapters of this book. Now here's an opportunity to get some hands-on practice. Follow these steps at your computer to produce the worksheet shown here. Steps include chapter numbers to help you find more information on the skills required. When formatting the sheet, remember that the available typefaces, sizes, and attributes can differ from one computer to the next, so your sheet may not match the one shown here in every detail.

Start 1-2-3 if it is not already running. Unless you already have a blank worksheet file on your screen, start a new file by clicking on File in the menu bar and then clicking on the New command. If the New File dialog box appears, verify that Create a plain worksheet is checked, and then click on OK. *Chapter 6*

File	
New	
Open...	Ctrl+O
Close	
Save	Ctrl+S
Save As...	
Doc Info...	
Protect...	
Send Mail...	
Print Preview...	
Page Setup...	
Print...	Ctrl+P
Printer Setup...	
Exit	
1 JUNE.WK4	
2 BONUS2.WK4	
3 SALARY.WK4	
4 VACATION.WK4	
5 WAGES.WK4	

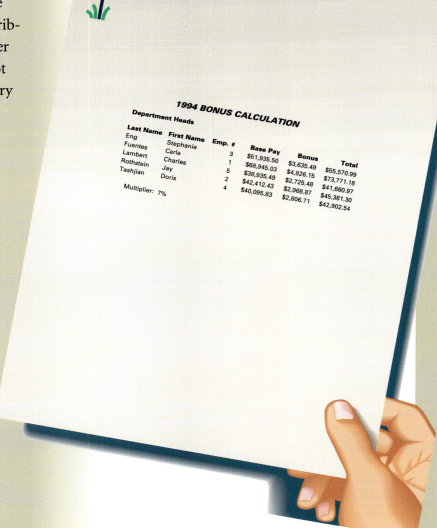

LawnBirds, Inc.

1994 BONUS CALCULATION
Department Heads

Last Name	First Name	Emp. #	Base Pay	Bonus	Total
Eng	Stephanie	3	$51,935.50	$3,635.49	$55,570.99
Fuentes	Carla	1	$68,945.03	$4,826.15	$73,771.18
Lambert	Charles	5	$38,935.49	$2,725.48	$41,660.97
Rothstein	Jay	2	$42,412.43	$2,968.87	$45,381.30
Tashjian	Doris	4	$40,095.83	$2,806.71	$42,902.54

Multiplier: 7%

Enter the basic sheet exactly as shown here. All numbers are plain data, not formula results. *Chapter 4*

Click on File in the menu bar and then click on the Save command to display the Save As dialog box. *Chapter 6*

In the File name text box, type **94bonus** and then click on OK to save the work-sheet file as 94BONUS.WK4. *Chapter 6*

Select the Base Pay numbers and the blank cells beneath the Bonus and Total headings (cells C6 through E10). *Chapter 5*

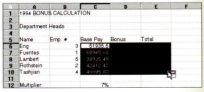

Click on Style in the menu bar and then click on the Number Format command to display the Number Format dialog box. *Chapter 9*

In the Format list, click on Currency. Verify that the Decimal places text box is set to 2 and that US Dollar is selected in the Currency list box. Then click on OK to apply this format to the numbers now in the Base Pay column and to the numbers that will later appear in the Bonus and Total columns. *Chapter 9*

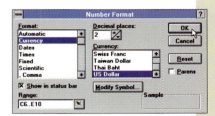

Move to cell D6, type **+c6*c12**, and click on the Confirm button. The dollar signs in this formula produce an absolute reference so that when you copy this formula to other cells, the reference to the multiplier in cell C12 will not change. *Chapter 10*

With cell D6 current, point to the bottom-right corner of the cell so that the mouse pointer assumes the drag-and-fill shape—a hollow arrow with two down-pointing and two right-pointing solid triangles. Then drag-and-fill the four cells below D6. Release the mouse button and observe that each filled-in cell multiplies the cell to its left by the multiplier in cell C12. *Chapter 10*

Continue to next page ▶

Continue below

 10

Move to cell E6 and enter the formula +**c6+d6** to calculate Eng's total

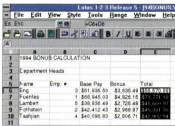

pay. Then, with cell E6 still current, drag-and-fill the four cells below it. *Chapter 10*

 11

Select the range A3..E5 (*Department Heads* through *Total*). Then click on Style in the menu

bar and click on the Font & Attributes command to display the Font & Attributes dialog box. *Chapter 9*

 12

In the Attributes area, check Bold. Then click on OK

to boldface the contents of the selected cells. *Chapter 9*

 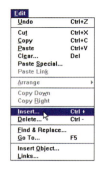 **13**

Move to any cell in column B. Then click on Edit in the menu bar and click on the Insert command to display the Insert dialog box. *Chapter 8*

 14

Click on Column and then click on OK to insert a new, blank column to

the left of the Emp. # column. *Chapter 8*

 15

As shown here, enter the contents of the newly created column B. Also, edit cell A5 to read *Last Name*. *Chapters 4 and 5*

	A	B	C
1	1994 BONUS CALCULATION		
2			
3	**Department Heads**		
4			
5	**Last Name**	**First Name**	**Emp. #**
6	Eng	Stephanie	3
7	Fuentes	Carla	1
8	Lambert	Charles	5
9	Rothstein	Jay	2
10	Tashjian	Doris	4

 16

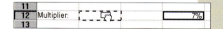

Move to cell D12, point to the cell border so that the mouse pointer assumes the shape of a hand. Then drag two cells to the left to move the cell contents to cell B12. *Chapter 8*

17

Select the range C5..F5 (*Emp. #* through *Total*), click on Style in the menu bar, and then click on the Alignment command to display the Alignment dialog box. *Chapter 9*

 18

Under Horizontal, click on the Right radio button, and then click on OK to right-align the contents of the selected cells. *Chapter 9*

 19

Using the same technique as in the two preceding steps, right-align cell A12 (*Multiplier:*), and left-align cell B12 (*7%*). Hint: To change the alignment of one cell, simply move to the cell; do not select a range. *Chapter 9*

 20

Move to cell A1 (*1994 Bonus Calculation*), click on Style in the menu bar, and then click on the Font & Attributes command. *Chapter 9*

 21

Click on 14 in the Size list, check Bold and Italics under Attributes, and then click on OK. *Chapter 9*

 22

Select the range A1..F1, click on Style in the menu bar, and then click on the Alignment command. *Chapter 9*

 23

Under Horizontal, click on the Center radio button and check Across columns, and then click on OK. *Chapter 9*

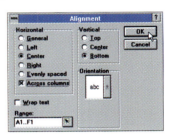

 24

If any column is too narrow to display its cell contents properly, point to the column letter's right edge until the mouse pointer changes to a double-headed arrow. Then drag to widen the column. Repeat this for any other columns that are too narrow. *Chapter 8*

 25

Resave the worksheet, print it if you want, and close it. *Chapter 6*

CHAPTER 12

Charts

You probably have a pretty good understanding of your worksheet data. (Well, you *should*!) But hand a worksheet printout to a colleague or show that worksheet to a client in a presentation and you may get a puzzled reaction. Columns and rows of numbers are not always the best way to give someone information at a glance.

That's where charts (often called *graphs*) come in. A good chart makes data visually meaningful. By emphasizing trends and comparative factors, a chart tells a story quickly and concisely. Remember the proverb "A picture is worth a thousand words"? If that's true, then a chart is easily worth a thousand *numbers*.

1-2-3 can graphically express all or part of your data in any one of several popular chart types. Plus, as you edit the data upon which the chart is based, 1-2-3 updates the chart automatically to reflect the new data. This chapter explains how to create a chart based on worksheet data, how to change a chart's type, and how to improve a chart's appearance by modifying its various elements.

How to Create a Chart

Creating a chart is surprisingly easy. Tell 1-2-3 which data you want the chart to plot, issue a single command, and then tell 1-2-3 where to put the chart. That's it! Once the chart is created, you can then modify it as you wish using the techniques shown on this and the next two pages.

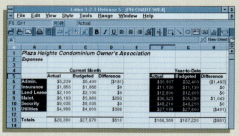

1 Select the data, column headings, and row headings you want to chart. Often, as shown here, you need to select a collection (see Chapter 5). Also, carefully consider whether you want to include rows and columns containing totals in the chart; frequently, you don't.

TIP SHEET

▶ When you create a chart, it becomes a part of your worksheet file. You can print it along with your worksheet data, or select and print only the chart itself. (See Chapter 7.)

▶ Note that a chart does not reside within a cell or cells. It's actually a *drawn object* that sits like a slip of paper on top of the worksheet. Because of this, a poorly placed or resized chart may overlap and obscure regular cell contents. A chart can even overlap other charts that reside on the same worksheet.

▶ Once you've created a chart, it maintains a link with the data you used to create that chart. If you edit a chart's underlying data, 1-2-3 updates the chart automatically.

▶ You can at once place and size a chart by dragging rather than clicking in step 3. As you drag, a dotted outline appears. Drag this outline to the desired size and then release the mouse button.

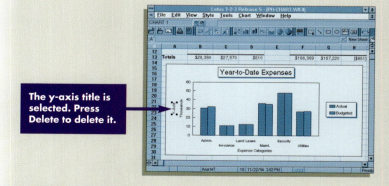

The y-axis title is selected. Press Delete to delete it.

7 To delete a title—or any chart element, for that matter—click on it to select it. Handles appear around just that element. Then, simply press the Delete key. Be careful! You can also delete the entire chart if that's what's selected.

2 Click on Tools in the menu bar, and then click on the Chart command.

3 The mouse pointer assumes the shape shown here, indicating that 1-2-3 is ready to place your chart. Scroll to a blank portion of your worksheet, or even to a new or existing sheet within the same worksheet file. Point to where you want the upper-left corner of your chart to be, and then click the mouse button.

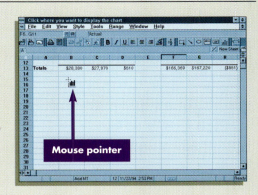

Mouse pointer

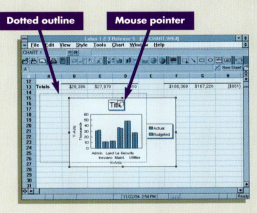

Dotted outline Mouse pointer

4 A bar chart appears where you clicked. (You'll learn how to change the chart's type on the next page.) If the chart's not where you want it, point to a blank area of the chart, near the edge, and then drag. As you drag, the mouse pointer changes to a fist. Using the dotted outline that appears as a guide, release the mouse button when the chart is in the location you want.

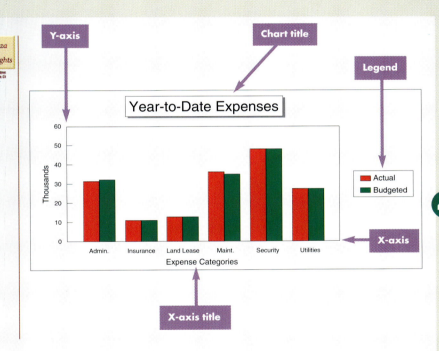

Y-axis

Chart title

Legend

Year-to-Date Expenses

X-axis

X-axis title

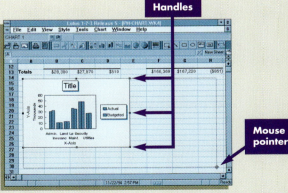

Handles

Mouse pointer

5 1-2-3 creates charts in a default size. To make the chart bigger or smaller, point to any one of the eight solid *handles* that appear along the chart's perimeter. When the mouse pointer changes to a four-headed arrow, drag inward to make the chart smaller or outward to make it larger. Using the dotted outline that appears as a guide, release the mouse button when the chart is the size you want.

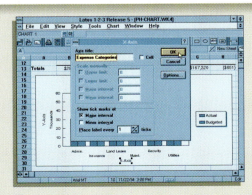

6 1-2-3 uses generic labels for your chart's title (*Title*) and axes titles (*Y-Axis* and *X-Axis*). To customize a title's wording, first double-click on it. Then, in the dialog box that appears, type the desired text in the selected text box and click on OK.

How to Change the Chart Type

Any given set of data is usually best illustrated by a single chart type. For example, a bar chart, as shown on the previous page, is ideal for comparing two data *series*—such as budgeted and actual expenditures—to each other. A pie chart, as shown on this page, is better for illustrating how various elements within a single data series—such as categories of expenditures within a single budget—compose an overall total. With 1-2-3's wide variety of chart types, you're bound to find a type that suits your data perfectly.

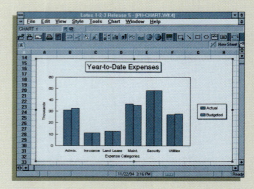

1 Select the chart you want to change. (Click in a blank area of the chart, away from any chart elements. When the chart is selected, handles will appear along the chart's perimeter.)

6 Click on OK.

2 Click on Chart in the menu bar, and then click on the Type command. (Observe that when a chart is selected, the Chart menu replaces the Range menu.)

3 1-2-3 offers 12 chart types, from line charts to three-dimensional pie charts. Under Types, click on the name of the chart type that best suits your data. If you're not familiar with chart-type names, just click on each name and look to the right of the Types area for graphical examples.

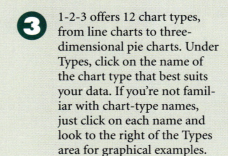
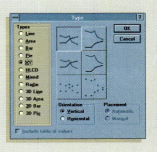

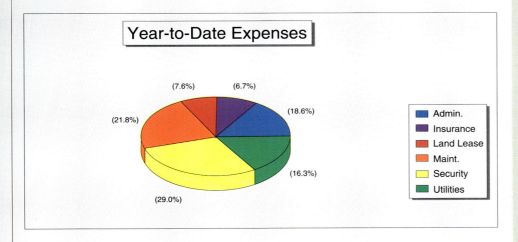

5 For most chart types, you can also choose an orientation. That is, you can swap the data between x and y axes, thus rotating your plotted data 90 degrees. (Because Pie, Radar, and 3D Pie charts have no axes, you can't change their orientation.)

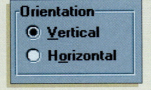

4 For most chart types, 1-2-3 offers multiple subtypes, or *styles*. For example, as shown here, you can have either one of two 3D Pie styles, one in which the data rotates counterclockwise, the other in which the data rotates clockwise. Click on the style that best suits your data.

How to Modify Chart Elements

O nce you've created a chart, added descriptive titles, and selected a chart type and style, your work may be done. Or maybe not. Perhaps there are still a few things that just aren't right with your chart. Maybe the chart title should be bigger and in a different typeface, or the numbers along an axis need to be formatted differently, or the colors don't print well. This page shows you some examples of how you can modify various chart elements. Note that many of the commands shown here are the same commands used in Chapter 9 to format worksheet cells.

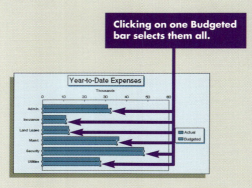

Clicking on one Budgeted bar selects them all.

▶ 1 Select the chart element you want to change. (Click on it so that handles appear around the element.) Note that some chart elements consist of many parts that will be formatted together. For example, if you click on one bar in a bar chart, every bar of the same color is selected; if you click on one number along an axis, every number is selected.

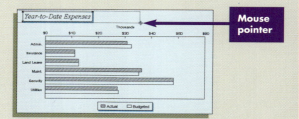

Mouse pointer

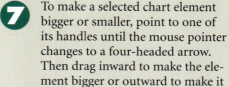

7 To make a selected chart element bigger or smaller, point to one of its handles until the mouse pointer changes to a four-headed arrow. Then drag inward to make the element bigger or outward to make it smaller.

2 If a selected chart element consists of text or numbers, you can change the typeface, size, attributes, and/or color. Click on Style in the menu bar, click

on the Font & Attributes command, set the desired typeface, size, attributes, and/or color, and then click on OK.

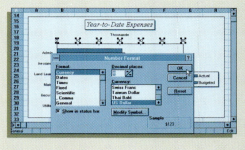

3 If a selected chart element consists of numbers, you can change its number format. Click on Style in the menu bar, click on the Number Format command, set the number-format options as desired, and then click on OK.

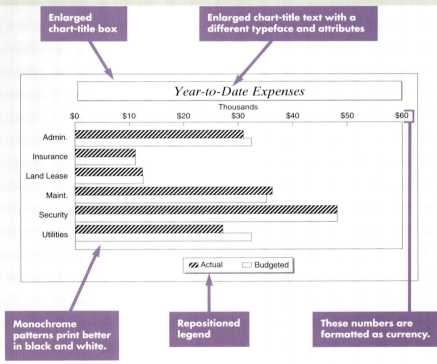

Enlarged chart-title box

Enlarged chart-title text with a different typeface and attributes

Monochrome patterns print better in black and white.

Repositioned legend

These numbers are formatted as currency.

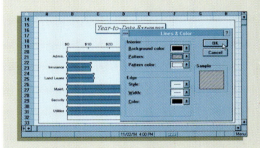

4 If the selected chart element is a graphical element—such as a line, box, bar, or pie slice—you can change its background and border. Click on Style in the menu bar, click on the Lines & Color command, set the background and border (Interior and Edge) options as desired, and then click on OK.

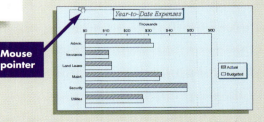

Mouse pointer

6 You can also use commands to move certain chart elements. To move the legend, for example, click on Chart in the menu bar, click on the Legend command, click on Right of plot or Below plot at the bottom of the Legend dialog box, and then click on OK.

5 To move a selected chart element, point to a blank area within the element and drag. As you drag, the mouse pointer changes to a fist, and a dotted outline shows you where the element will be placed should you release the mouse button at that moment. (Note that some elements only move as a set.)

CHAPTER 13

Finding Data

 Although many people use worksheets strictly for "number crunching," 1-2-3 worksheets can also be used as *electronic databases* to store related sets of data.

You've probably worked with databases—though perhaps not electronic ones—for years: telephone books, personnel records, and inventories, for example. People and businesses have put many databases on computers because computers make data easier to find, sort, edit, and so on.

This chapter and the next focus on two of 1-2-3's database management capabilities: finding and sorting. In this chapter, you'll learn two ways to find data. You'll learn how to find all the records that meet a certain criterion—to find every client who's based in North Carolina, for example. You'll also learn how to use specific characters to find a single record—for example, using *Smith* to locate the record for an employee who lives on Smith Level Road.

Before proceeding, note these fundamental database terms: A *record* is all the data about one subject; for example, all the personnel data about Kat Moran or all the sales information about one product. A *field* is a data category. For example, fields in a personnel database might include employee name, date of hire, and pay rate. In standard databases such as those shown in this book, each record is one row and each field is one column. The field (column) headings are called *field names*.

How to Find a Set of Records

To find a specific set of records, you give 1-2-3 a *criterion* against which to test every record in the database. For example, a criterion might instruct 1-2-3 to find only those records where the department name is Training. 1-2-3 selects only those records that meet your criterion. Once selected, it's a simple matter to print, edit, or specially format those records—whatever meets your needs.

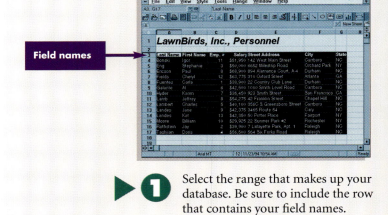

Field names

TIP SHEET

▶ Depending on your data, you may be able in step 4 to select the value you need from the Value drop-down list rather than typing that value. The Value list will contain every value contained in the field you specified in step 3.

▶ If you plan to find records regularly in a specific database, it may be helpful to give that database range a name to make selecting it more convenient. To name a range, select it (in our example, we would select cells A3 to G17), click on Range in the menu bar, and then click on Name. Type a name for your range (for example, *Personnel Records*), and then click on OK. Now, anytime you need to select that range in preparation for finding a set of records, click on Edit in the menu bar, click on Go To, and then double-click on your range's name.

▶① Select the range that makes up your database. Be sure to include the row that contains your field names.

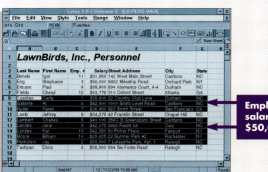

Employees whose salary is less than $50,000

 7 1-2-3 selects only those records that meet your criterion. Scroll as necessary to view every selected record.

 Observe the Criteria box to make sure that the criterion you set is correct, and then click on OK.

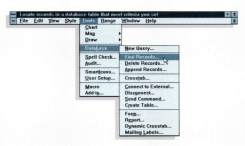

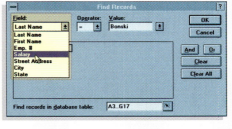

2 Click on Tools in the menu bar, click on Database, and then click on the Find Records command.

3 Open the Field drop-down list and click on the name of the field for which you will test data. (1-2-3 gets this list of field names from the first row of the range you selected in step 1.) For example, if you want to find in a personnel database every record for employees who are in a specific salary range, click on the name of the field that contains salary information.

LawnBirds, Inc., Personnel

Last Name	First Name	Emp. #	Salary	Street Address	City	State
Bonski	Igor	11	$51,950	142 West Main Street	Carrboro	NC
Eng	Stephanie	3	$50,000	6652 Milestrip Road	Orchard park	NY
Ericson	Paul	8	$68,900	894 Alamance Court, A-4	Durham	NC
Fields	Cheryl	12	$63,775	310 Oxford Street	Atlanta	GA
Fuentes	Carla	1	$38,900	22 Country Club Lane	Durham	NC
Galante	Al	6	$42,500	1000 Smith Level Road	Carrboro	NC
Hyder	Karen	7	$36,450	923 Smith Street	San Francisco	CA
Lamb	Jeffrey	8	$54,275	42 Franklin Street	Chapel Hill	NC
Lambert	Charles	5	$40,100	356C S Greensboro Street	Carrboro	NC
Landes	Jane	9	$42,375	3465 Route 54	Cary	NC
Landes	Kat	13	$42,350	50 Potter Place	Fairport	NY
Moore	Billiam	10	$29,925	22 Sumner Park #2	Rochester	NY
Rothstein	Jay	2	$39,900	7 Lafayette Park, Apt 1	Raleigh	NC
Tashjian	Doris	4	$56,500	564 Six Forks Road	Raleigh	NC

Chris,
I need a printout of just the employees who make less than $50,000/year.
Thanks!
-Kat

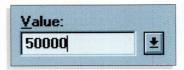

4 In the Value box, type the text or number that will constitute your data test. For example, to find records of those employees who earn under $50,000, type **50000**. (Number formatting is optional; *50000* or *$50,000* would yield the same results.)

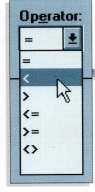

5 Open the Operator drop-down list and click on the comparison operator that specifies the manner in which the field you specified in step 3 should be tested against the value you typed in step 4. All standard operators are available: equal to (=), less than (<), greater than (>), less than or equal to (<=), greater than or equal to (>=), and not equal to (<>). In our example, we would choose < to find every employee who earns less than $50,000.

How to Find a Specific Record

Sometimes you don't need to find an entire set of records. Sometimes, you instead need to find a *specific* record. For example, what if you need to edit a specific employee's salary? In a small worksheet file, this may not be problem. But what if your personnel records are stored in a very large file? With 256 columns and 8,192 rows per worksheet and up to 256 sheets per file, your worksheet file could contain 536,870,912 cells. Talk about finding a needle in a haystack! Fortunately, 1-2-3's Find & Replace command makes the task practically effortless.

▶ **1** Open the worksheet file that contains the record you're seeking. *Only* if you know the record is in a specific range, select that range. (Sorry, no collections allowed.) As you might expect, 1-2-3 can search much faster through a range than an entire worksheet file.

8 If 1-2-3 has located the record you wanted, click on Close to close the Find dialog box; you are now free to edit the record as necessary. If your search characters are stored more than once in the worksheet file or specified range, however, you may need to click on Find Next one or more times to find the correct record. Once you do, click on Close.

TIP SHEET

▶ If you click on Find Next (step 8) after 1-2-3 has found every occurrence of your specified characters, 1-2-3 displays the message *No more matching strings*. Click on OK to clear this message.

▶ As the name implies, the Find & Replace command can also be used to replace characters that you find. For online help on replacing characters, click on the Find & Replace dialog box's question-mark icon (see Chapter 11).

▶ Unlike the Find Records command (described on the previous page), you cannot use the Find & Replace command to find values— either as numbers that you've typed (unless 1-2-3 sees those numbers as text, such as in a street address) or as formula results. For example, if the result of the formula @SUM(D6..D11) is 125, Find & Replace will not locate this formula if you specify "125." It *will* find the formula, however, if you specify "@SUM" or "(D6..D11)".

2 Click on Edit in the menu bar and then click on the Find & Replace command.

3 In the Search for text box, type the characters you want to use for your search. For example, if you know that an employee's first name is Karen, type *Karen* or *karen* (case is irrelevant). Because 1-2-3 searches for the specified characters regardless of whether those characters form a complete word or not, you could even type *kar* or *ren*.

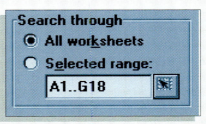

4 Under Search through, click on All worksheets to have 1-2-3 search through the entire worksheet file. To instead have 1-2-3 search only through the range you selected in step 1 (if any), click on Selected range.

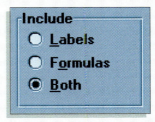

5 If you know that the characters you typed in the Search for text box are part of a label (text), click on Labels in the Include box. If you know those characters are part of a formula, click on Formulas. Otherwise, leave Both selected.

6 Click on OK.

Chris-

Here's the address of the new employee, Karen:

564 Weaver Street
Carrboro, NC

-Doris

First occurrence of "Karen"

7 1-2-3 searches your worksheet file or specified range column by column, starting with the leftmost column. If you're searching the entire worksheet file, 1-2-3 starts its search on the first sheet and continues to other sheets as necessary. When 1-2-3 finds the characters you specified, it opens the Find dialog box and moves to the cell containing those characters. (If 1-2-3 *cannot* find the characters you specified, it displays the message *String not found*.)

CHAPTER 14

Sorting Data

 Most data is easier to work with and more presentable when there is some sense to the sequence of rows. For example, personnel lists often are arranged alphabetically by employees' last names.

You might try building a worksheet in the sequence you need, but as you add, delete, and edit data, it's bound to fall out of order. Moving rows around to restore order could be quite grueling. Instead, use 1-2-3's highly capable Sort command. It can sort your data instantly according to the content of any column or columns you choose.

Some terminology: A sort *key* is the column whose content is the basis for the sort. For example, if a personnel list contains columns for last name, Social Security number, salary, and hire date, and you sort the rows according to salary, the salary column is the sort key. 1-2-3 allows you unlimited keys per sort, although most people rarely need more than three keys at a time. When the first key results in a tie—for example, when two or more employees have the same salary—the optional second key kicks in, perhaps sorting by last name those employees with identical salaries. An optional third key could sort by Social Security number any employees who have both the same salary and the same last name.

By default, 1-2-3 sorts in *ascending* order: lowest to highest for numbers and alphabetical (A–Z) order for text. However, you can specify a *descending* sort—for example, arranging employees from highest to lowest by salary or Z–A by last name.

How to Sort Data

Sorting data involves telling 1-2-3 what to sort, what keys to use, and whether to sort in ascending or descending order. As you'll see, the Sort command, while easy to issue, subjects you to certain pitfalls and makes quite significant changes to your worksheet. Though you should always be careful when working with important data, be especially cautious when setting up a sort operation. You can reverse a sort with the Undo command (see Chapter 11), but only if you catch your mistake before performing another action.

TIP SHEET

▶ Save your worksheet immediately before performing a sort. That way, if the sort goes awry and you notice the problem too late to perform an undo, you can close the worksheet without saving it and then reopen it (see Chapter 6). The reopened worksheet will be exactly as you last saved it—before the defective sort.

▶ If you or another user has done any sorting in the current worksheet file, sort keys may already be set up when you open the Sort dialog box (see step 3). If these keys are set up the way you want, skip to step 7. Otherwise, click on the Reset button to clear the existing keys and then continue with step 3.

▶ Note this important difference when selecting records for a sort versus selecting them to find records (see Chapter 13): When finding records, you *do* select the field names (column headings); when sorting records, you *don't*.

These records currently are sorted in descending order by number of employees.

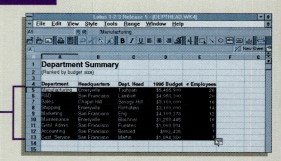

▶ **1** Select the data you want to sort. Be sure to select entire data records; only selected cells are moved in a sort, so if you select partial rows, some cells in a record will shift while others stay put. Do *not* select field names or any other type of headings lest they be sorted, too.

8 Immediately inspect the sort results. If you did not get the results you expected—maybe in step 1 you mistakenly selected incomplete records—click on Edit in the menu bar, and then click on the Undo command. This will reverse your sort operation so that you can start over from scratch.

"If the first key (budget figures) results in any ties, sort the ties using column A (department names) as the key."

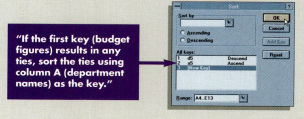

7 Click on OK to perform the sort.

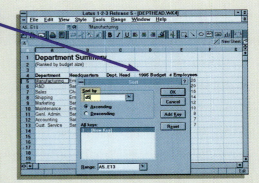

Column D contains the budget figures.

2 Click on Range in the menu bar, and then click on the Sort command.

3 In the Sort By text box, type the address of any cell in the column that you want to use as your first key (unless an appropriate cell address is already displayed there). For example, if you want to sort by budget amounts stored in column D, type *d1*, *d5*, or any column D cell address. If you can't see which columns contain what data, move the Sort dialog box (drag its title bar) as we have done here.

Departments with the same budget are sorted in alphabetical order.

LawnBirds, Inc.

Department Summary
(Ranked by budget size)

Department	Headquarters	Dept. Head	1995 Budget	# Employees
Manufacturing	Emeryville	Tashjian	$5,465,900	26
R&D	San Francisco	Lambert	$4,958,300	20
Marketing	San Francisco	Eng	$4,109,373	12
Sales	Chapel Hill	Savage-Hill	$3,100,000	16
Shipping	Emeryville	Rothstein	$3,100,000	14
Cust. Service	San Francisco	Martin	$1,691,638	7
Maintenance	Emeryville	Blochner	$1,258,445	10
Genl. Admin.	San Francisco	Fuentes	$1,009,894	8
Accounting	San Francisco	Bernard	$902,435	7

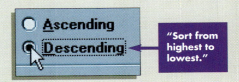

"Sort from highest to lowest."

4 By default, 1-2-3 sorts in ascending order. If you want this key to sort in descending order, mark the Descending radio button.

5 Click on the Add Key button.

6 To set additional keys to break ties produced by your first key, repeat steps 3 through 5 as desired. 1-2-3 adds each of your keys to the All keys list box.

TRY IT!

Here's a chance to sharpen the 1-2-3 skills you've developed throughout this book. Follow the steps given to produce the printout shown here. Remember that the available typefaces, sizes, attributes, and colors can differ from one computer and printer to the next, so your printout may not match this one in every detail. Chapter numbers are included to help you find more information on the skills required for each step.

Start a new worksheet file and save it as BESTSELL.WK4. *Chapter 6*

Flamingo Sales

Product Name	1Q Sales	2Q Sales
Classic Pink	$964,079.07	$1,156,894.88
Coral Gables	$510,125.36	$739,681.77
Econo-Bird	$1,230,250.72	$1,968,401.15
Old Reliable	$285,438.76	$533,770.48
The Acrobat	$55,062.68	$110,125.36
Wingspan	$887,656.70	$1,553,399.23
Yard Monarch	$453,953.71	$385,860.65

2

	A	B	C
1	Flamingo Sales		
2			
3	Product Name	1Q Sales	2Q Sales
4	Wingspan	$887,656.70	$1,553,399.23
5	Coral Gables	$510,125.36	$739,681.77
6	Old Reliable	$285,438.76	$533,770.48
7	The Acrobat	$55,062.68	$110,125.36
8	Classic Pink	$964,079.07	$1,156,894.88
9	Yard Monarch	$453,953.71	$385,860.65
10	Econo-Bird	$1,230,250.72	$1,968,401.15

Enter the basic, unformatted worksheet shown here. All numbers are plain data, not formula results. Widen columns by dragging each column letter's right edge as needed to see each cell's complete contents. *Chapters 4 and 8*

3

	A	B	C
1	*Flamingo Sales*		
2			
3	**Product Name**	**1Q Sales**	**2Q Sales**
4	Wingspan	$887,656.70	$1,553,399.23
5	Coral Gables	$510,125.36	$739,681.77
6	Old Reliable	$285,438.76	$533,770.48
7	The Acrobat	$55,062.68	$110,125.36
8	Classic Pink	$964,079.07	$1,156,894.88
9	Yard Monarch	$453,953.71	$385,860.65
10	Econo-Bird	$1,230,250.72	$1,968,401.15

Format cell A1 (*Flamingo Sales*) as Times New Roman 18-point bold italic, the range A3..C3 (the field names) as Times New Roman 12-point bold, and the range A4..C10 (the remainder of the database) as Times New Roman 12-point. When done, drag the right column borders to widen columns as needed. *Chapters 8 and 9*

4

	A	B	C
1	*Flamingo Sales*		
2			
3	**Product Name**	**1Q Sales**	**2Q Sales**
4	Wingspan	$887,656.70	$1,553,399.23
5	Coral Gables	$510,125.36	$739,681.77
6	Old Reliable	$285,438.76	$533,770.48
7	The Acrobat	$55,062.68	$110,125.36
8	Classic Pink	$964,079.07	$1,156,894.88
9	Yard Monarch	$453,953.71	$385,860.65
10	Econo-Bird	$1,230,250.72	$1,968,401.15

Select and right-align the range B3..C3 (*1Q Sales* and *2Q Sales*). Reminder: Select the Alignment command from the Style menu. *Chapters 5 and 9*

5

Select the range A4..B10 (the database records). *Chapter 5*

6

Range
Version...
Fill...
Fill by Example
Sort...
Parse...
Transpose...
Name...
Analyze ▶

Click on Range and then click on Sort. *Chapter 14*

7

Verify that *A4* is displayed in the Sort by text box. If it isn't, then type **a4** to replace the current address. *Chapter 14*

8

Verify that Ascending is marked, and then click on Add Key. *Chapter 14*

9

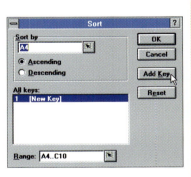

	A	B	C
1	*Flamingo Sales*		
2			
3	**Product Name**	**1Q Sales**	**2Q Sales**
4	Classic Pink	$964,079.07	$1,156,894.88
5	Coral Gables	$510,125.36	$739,681.77
6	Econo-Bird	$1,230,250.72	$1,968,401.15
7	Old Reliable	$285,438.76	$533,770.48
8	The Acrobat	$55,062.68	$110,125.36
9	Wingspan	$887,656.70	$1,553,399.23
10	Yard Monarch	$453,953.71	$385,860.65

Click on OK to sort the database records by product name. *Chapter 14*

Continue to next page ▶

TRY IT!

Continue below

 10

Select the range A3..C10 (the database records *and* field names). *Chapter 5*

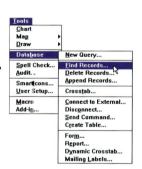

11

Click on Tools, click on Database, and then click on Find Records. *Chapter 13*

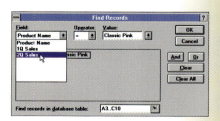

12

From the Field drop-down list, select 2Q Sales. *Chapter 13*

 13

In the Value box, type **1,000,000**. *Chapter 13*

 14

From the Operator drop-down list, select >. *Chapter 13*

 15

Verify that *2Q Sales> 1,000,000* is displayed in the Criteria box, and then click on OK to select the three records where second-quarter sales exceed $1,000,000. *Chapter 13*

16

Add the range B3..C3 (*1Q Sales* and *2Q Sales*) to the current selection. Reminder: Hold down the Ctrl key as you drag over or click on the cells. *Chapter 5*

17

Click on Tools and then click on Chart. *Chapter 12*

18

Point to the left edge of cell A12 and then click to place the chart. *Chapter 12*

19

Scroll as necessary to bring the entire chart into view, and then double-click on the chart title (*Title*). *Chapter 12*

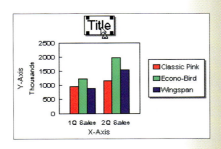

20

In the top text box, type **Our Best-Selling Birds**, and then click on OK. *Chapter 12*

21

Select and delete both axis labels (*Y-Axis* and *X-Axis*). *Chapter 12*

22

Select the chart's y-axis numbers. *Chapter 12*

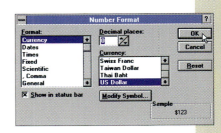

23

Click on Style and then click on Number Format.

24

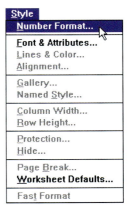

Click on Currency in the Format list box, set the Decimal places box to 0, verify that US Dollar is selected in the Currency list, and then click on OK.

25

Save, print, and close the worksheet file.

CHAPTER 15

Shortcuts

Did you ever ask for driving directions in an unfamiliar city? The less familiar you were with the territory, the more likely you wanted to know the easiest, least confusing way to go—even if it wasn't the fastest. Only when you are comfortable with the general layout of a city are you interested in shortcuts.

Learning to use software is a similar experience. That's why this book really isn't about shortcuts. Because you started out as an inexperienced user, this book has assumed you want to know one way—the most straightforward way—to get the job done.

But now that you are comfortable with 1-2-3, you are ready to sample the many convenient shortcuts available from its status bar and SmartIcons. Some of these shortcuts can save you considerable effort over the long run and are certainly worth the time it takes to learn about them. Others—shortcuts that address tasks you perform infrequently—you may want to skip. Use of the status bar and SmartIcons is entirely optional.

How to Format Cells from the Status Bar

As you learned in Chapter 3, the status bar sits along the bottom of the 1-2-3 application window. You may have noticed that the formatting buttons in the left half of the status bar often display information about the formatting of the current or selected cells. You can use these buttons to change cell formatting, thus sparing you frequent trips to the Style menu (see Chapter 9).

 1 The *format selector* displays the number format of the current or selected cells. To change that format, click on the format selector and then click on the desired format's name.

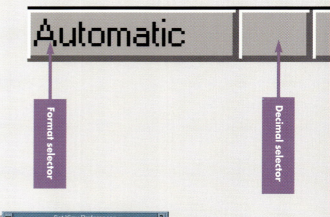

▶ **When multiple cells are selected, each formatting button displays information only if that particular formatting is the same across the entire selection. Otherwise, the button is blank. For example, if you select two cells, one formatted as Arial 12-point and the other as Arial 18-point, the font selector will display *Arial*, but the point-size selector will be blank.**

▶ **Even when a formatting button is blank as described above, you can still use it as described on this page to format cells.**

▶ **Note that by combining certain number formats with popular settings, the format selector provides a more convenient (albeit less exhaustive) list of number-format options than the Number Format dialog box you learned about in Chapter 9. For example, rather than choosing Currency and then the British Pound currency symbol separately, you simply click on British Pound.**

▶ **Another often useful status-bar button, the SmartIcons selector, is described on the next page.**

 6 Next, clear the Status bar check box at the bottom of the Set View Preferences dialog box and click on OK.

2 If the number format of the current or selected cells supports decimal places, the *decimal selector* displays the current decimal setting. To change this setting, click on the decimal selector and then click on the desired number of decimal places.

3 The *font selector* displays the typeface of the current or selected cells. To change the typeface, click on the font selector, scroll as necessary, and then click on the desired typeface's name.

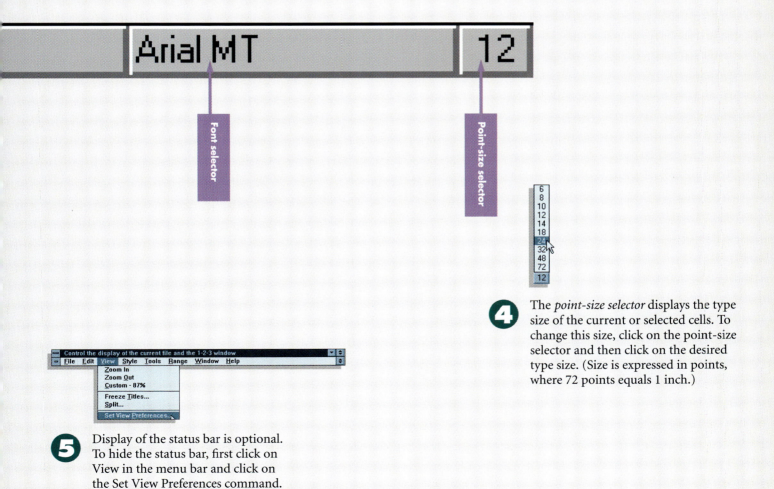

4 The *point-size selector* displays the type size of the current or selected cells. To change this size, click on the point-size selector and then click on the desired type size. (Size is expressed in points, where 72 points equals 1 inch.)

5 Display of the status bar is optional. To hide the status bar, first click on View in the menu bar and click on the Set View Preferences command.

How to Use SmartIcons to Issue Commands

As you learned in Chapter 3, a set of Smart-Icons sits across the top of the 1-2-3 work area, directly below the edit line. These SmartIcons are buttons that serve as one-click shortcuts for many common 1-2-3 commands you might otherwise issue from menus. This page describes only those SmartIcons that provide shortcuts to tasks covered in this book. Chapter numbers show you where that task was covered.

▶**❶** Click on the *Open an existing file* SmartIcon as a shortcut for clicking on Open in the File menu. Click on the *Save the current file* SmartIcon as a shortcut for clicking on Save in the File menu. *Chapter 6*

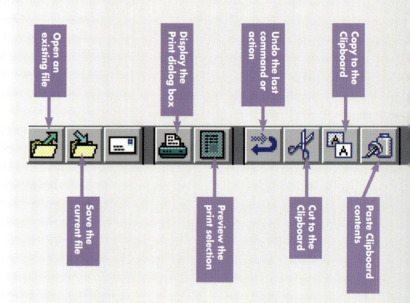

❽ Click on the *Draw a chart using the selected range* SmartIcon as a shortcut for clicking on Chart in the Tools menu. *Chapter 12*

❼ Click on the *Sum values above or to the left* SmartIcon to have 1-2-3 automatically create a formula that sums the numbers above or to the left of the current cell. Check this formula carefully to make sure that 1-2-3 created the formula you wanted. *Chapter 4*

2 Click on the *Display the Print dialog box* SmartIcon as a shortcut for clicking on Print in the File menu. Click on the *Preview the print selection* SmartIcon as a shortcut for clicking on Print in the File menu and then clicking on the Preview button (or for clicking on Print Preview in the File menu). *Chapter 7*

3 Click on the *Undo the last command or action* SmartIcon as a shortcut for clicking on Undo in the Edit menu. *Chapter 11*

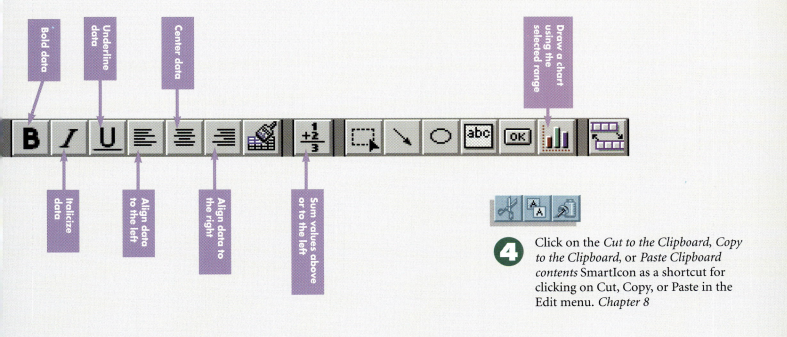

Bold data

Underline data

Center data

Draw a chart using the selected range

Italicize data

Align data to the left

Align data to the right

Sum values above or to the left

4 Click on the *Cut to the Clipboard*, *Copy to the Clipboard*, or *Paste Clipboard contents* SmartIcon as a shortcut for clicking on Cut, Copy, or Paste in the Edit menu. *Chapter 8*

6 Click on the *Align data to the left*, *Center data*, or *Align data to the right* SmartIcon as a shortcut for clicking on Alignment in the Style menu, selecting one of those horizontal alignments in the Alignment dialog box, and then clicking on OK. *Chapter 9*

5 Click on the *Bold data*, *Italicize data*, or *Underline data* SmartIcon as a shortcut for clicking on Font & Attributes in the Style menu, selecting one of those attributes in the Font & Attributes dialog box, and then clicking on OK. *Chapter 9*

APPENDIX

Installation

Software is not built into your computer; it is a separate product that someone has to buy and install. In many office situations, an administrator is responsible for installing software on users' machines. Likewise, computers purchased from stores and mail-order firms often come with software such as 1-2-3 already installed. Thus, there is a good chance that someone has installed 1-2-3 on your machine, and you can skip this appendix.

If you are not sure whether 1-2-3 is installed on your computer, follow the steps in Chapter 3 of this book. If you can start 1-2-3, then, plainly, it has been installed.

Lotus provides clear, complete installation instructions with 1-2-3. These instructions are more than sufficient for most computer users. Moreover, once you start the installation process, you will see on-screen instructions telling you what to do.

This appendix clarifies some of the installation issues that can slow down people who have little computer experience. It gives you the extra knowledge you may need to follow a generally straightforward procedure.

Tips on Installing 1-2-3

The basic installation procedure is simple: You place a disk from your 1-2-3 package in a disk drive, and your computer copies information from that disk onto your computer's hard disk. Then you place another disk in the disk drive, the computer copies more information, and so on until the hard disk holds the entire 1-2-3 program. There are quite a few variables in the installation process—so many that this book could not possibly discuss them all. Rest assured, however, that for most users in most situations, installation proceeds very smoothly. And the absolute worst thing that can happen if you make a mistake during installation is that you'll have to start over.

TIP SHEET

▶ Even if you received a shrink-wrapped copy of 1-2-3 with your computer, 1-2-3 may already be installed. That's because it is more convenient—and perfectly legal—for computer suppliers to install software using an already open copy rather than the copy they give you.

▶ If your computer has two floppy-disk drives of the same size, you can install 1-2-3 from either one. Be sure to use the same drive, though, throughout the installation process.

▶ Your computer may be set up to start Windows automatically when you switch it on. In this case you will see the Program Manager somewhere on your screen. Instead of exiting Windows to display the DOS prompt and perform step 4, click on File in the Program Manager menu bar, click on the Run command, type `a:\install` or `b:\install` depending on what floppy-disk drive holds the Install disk, and finally click on the OK button.

Make sure the disk fits the floppy-disk drive.

▶ **1** Your copy of 1-2-3 is on either 3.5-inch hard-cased disks or 5.25-inch soft-cased disks. To hold these disks during installation, your computer may have one 3.5-inch floppy-disk drive, one 5.25-inch floppy-disk drive, two drives of the same size, or—the most convenient arrangement—one drive of each size. Contact your software supplier if you don't have a floppy-disk drive of the correct size to accommodate your 1-2-3 disks.

9 As your computer restarts, take the last installation disk out of your floppy-disk drive and put it in a safe place with the other disks. Once your computer has successfully restarted, you can use 1-2-3. Proceed to Chapter 3 of this book—or first read Chapters 1 and 2 for some background information on DOS, Windows, and electronic spreadsheets in general.

8 As the 1-2-3 installation program nears completion, it will ask you for permission to update your computer's AUTOEXEC.BAT file, a special file your computer uses to decide what to do when it first turns on. Unless you're a computer expert, go ahead and click on Yes and then on Restart in the next dialog box to enable the AUTOEXEC.BAT changes to take effect.

7 It will take a while for your computer to read information from all the installation disks. When it's time for you to take out one disk and put in another, your computer will beep at you and tell you what disk it needs. After putting in the next disk, click on OK.

2 You need to know the *drive letter* of the floppy-disk drive you'll be using to install 1-2-3. If your computer has only one floppy-disk drive, it is drive A. If your computer has two floppy-disk drives, the top or left drive is probably drive A and the bottom or right drive is probably drive B.

Drive A **Drive B**

3 One of your 1-2-3 disks is labeled *Disk 1 Install*. To start the installation process, switch on your computer, wait a few moments for the computer to warm up, and insert the Install disk in the appropriate floppy-disk drive.

```
C:\>win b:\install
```

4 With the DOS prompt displayed on your computer screen, type **win a:\install** if the Install disk is in drive A, or **win b:\install** if the Install disk is in drive B. Then press the Enter key.

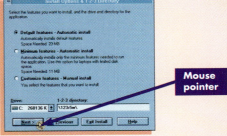

Mouse pointer

Default button

6 What if you see a question that you don't understand—and there's no computer expert around to help? Just leave everything as it is and click on the *default button*, the on-screen button with a darkened border. This will give your computer the answer Lotus thinks you probably want to give, and it's always an answer that can't do your computer any harm.

5 Sit and wait as information is copied from the installation disk to your computer's hard disk. Periodically you will be asked questions about how you want to install 1-2-3. These questions vary according to such factors as your computer equipment and the amount of empty space on your hard disk. To answer a question, find the answer on the screen and click on it. To *click* on an item means to roll the mouse on a flat surface until the on-screen *mouse pointer* is over the item and then press and immediately release the left mouse button.

INDEX

SYMBOLS

@functions
  @AVG, 87
  cases for naming, 86
  function selector, 86
  @MAX, 87
  @MIN, 87
  and shifted data, 64
  @SUM, 28–29, 86
  uses of, 28
' (apostrophe), preceding labels, 80
$ (dollar sign), preceding cell reference, 90, 91
+ (plus sign), preceding formulas, 27

A

absolute references, 90–91
active cell. *See* current cell
active window, 11
alignment
  cells, 80, 81, 82, 83
  for headings, 82–83
  numbers, 24
  text, 24
  with SmartIcons, 131
Alignment dialog box, 81
alphabetizing, 64
anchoring corner cell, when selecting ranges, 38
apostrophe ('), preceding labels, 80
arrow keys
  for data entry, 24
  for editing within a cell, 35
  for moving within ranges, 38
  and radio buttons, 16
  scrolling with, 15
  for selecting ranges, 38
Attributes options, 75

AUTOEXEC.BAT file, 134
automatic data recalculation, 3, 34, 35
Automatic number format, 76
automatic reference adjustment, 88

B

background
  adding, 79
  in charts, 111
  printing, 78
  removing, 78
bar chart, 107, 108
blank row, inserting, 65
border
  adding, 79
  in charts, 111
  printing, 78
  removing, 78
  thick, for totals, 78

C

Cancel button, 25
cell
  absolute reference for, 90, 91
  address. *See* cell address
  alignment, 80, 81, 82, 83
  background, 78, 79
  border, 78, 79
  changing color, 74
  clearing, 66
  copying, 68, 94
  current. *See* current cell
  decimal place in, 76
  defined, 2, 3, 20
  deleting, 66, 67
  deleting error from, 25
  displaying content of, 70
  dollar sign ($) in, 76, 90, 91

  dragging, 68–69
  editing content of, 34–35
  erasing content of, 34
  formatting content of, 74–75
  insertion point display, 34, 35
  moving, 68–69
  pointer, 20
  replacing content of, 35, 66
  selecting, 25
  selecting ranges, 38–39
  shifting, 66, 67
  Wrap Text option for, 80
cell address
  defined, 20
  for printing cell content, 56
  and sorting, 121
cell content. *See also* cell
  editing, 34–35
  modifying, 35
  recalculating formulas, 34
  replacing, 35
cell reference. *See also* cell address
  and cases, 26, 29
  defined, 27
  drag-and-fill adjustment for, 88, 89
  mixing adjacent and nonadjacent, 28
Chart command, 107
chart handles, 106, 107, 108
charts. *See also* bar chart; pie chart
  changing size of, 107
  creating, 106–107
  deleting elements from, 106
  dragging, 106, 107
  as drawn object, 106
  formatting, 110

See.

It's that simple.

Just open these colorfully illustrated guide-books and watch the answers to your software questions unfold.

The HOW TO USE books from Ziff-Davis Press make computing easy by presenting each task visually on two facing pages. You'll see what you want to achieve, and exactly how to achieve it.

There's no guess work. The HOW TO USE books are the affordable alternative for those of us who would rather let the computer do the work.

For more information call (800) 688-0448, ext. 253. For Corporate/ Government programs, call (800) 488-8741 ext. 297. For Education programs, call (800) 786-6541.

There is a book for every major software package, with new titles publishing every month.

ISBN: 1-56276-214-1
Price: $17.95

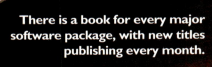

ISBN: 1-56276-185-4
Price: $17.95

ISBN: 1-56276-222-2
Price: $17.95

© 1994
Ziff-Davis Press

Ziff-Davis Press Survey of Readers

Please help us in our effort to produce the best books on personal computing.
For your assistance, we would be pleased to send you a FREE catalog
featuring the complete line of Ziff-Davis Press books.

1. How did you first learn about this book?

Recommended by a friend . . . . ☐ -1 (5)

Recommended by store personnel . . . . ☐ -2

Saw in Ziff-Davis Press catalog . . . . ☐ -3

Received advertisement in the mail . . . . ☐ -4

Saw the book on bookshelf at store . . . . ☐ -5

Read book review in: _____ ☐ -6

Saw an advertisement in: _____ ☐ -7

Other (Please specify): _____ ☐ -8

2. Which THREE of the following factors most influenced your decision to purchase this book? (Please check up to THREE.)

Front or back cover information on book . . . ☐ -1 (6)

Logo of magazine affiliated with book . . . . . . ☐ -2

Special approach to the content . . . . ☐ -3

Completeness of content . . . . ☐ -4

Author's reputation. ☐ -5

Publisher's reputation . . . . ☐ -6

Book cover design or layout . . . . ☐ -7

Index or table of contents of book . . . . ☐ -8

Price of book . . . . ☐ -9

Special effects, graphics, illustrations . . . . ☐ -0

Other (Please specify): _____ ☐ -x

3. How many computer books have you purchased in the last six months? _____ (7-10)

4. On a scale of 1 to 5, where 5 is excellent, 4 is above average, 3 is average, 2 is below average, and 1 is poor, please rate each of the following aspects of this book below. (Please circle your answer.)

Depth/completeness of coverage	5	4	3	2	1	(11)
Organization of material	5	4	3	2	1	(12)
Ease of finding topic	5	4	3	2	1	(13)
Special features/time saving tips	5	4	3	2	1	(14)
Appropriate level of writing	5	4	3	2	1	(15)
Usefulness of table of contents	5	4	3	2	1	(16)
Usefulness of index	5	4	3	2	1	(17)
Usefulness of accompanying disk	5	4	3	2	1	(18)
Usefulness of illustrations/graphics	5	4	3	2	1	(19)
Cover design and attractiveness	5	4	3	2	1	(20)
Overall design and layout of book	5	4	3	2	1	(21)
Overall satisfaction with book	5	4	3	2	1	(22)

5. Which of the following computer publications do you read regularly; that is, 3 out of 4 issues?

Byte . . . . ☐ -1 (23)

Computer Shopper . . . . ☐ -2

Corporate Computing . . . . ☐ -3

Dr. Dobb's Journal . . . . ☐ -4

LAN Magazine . . . . ☐ -5

MacWEEK . . . . ☐ -6

MacUser . . . . ☐ -7

PC Computing . . . . ☐ -8

PC Magazine . . . . ☐ -9

PC WEEK . . . . ☐ -0

Windows Sources . . . . ☐ -x

Other (Please specify): _____ ☐ -y

Please turn page.

6. What is your level of experience with personal computers? With the subject of this book?

	With PCs	With subject of book
Beginner.	☐ -1 (24)	☐ -1 (25)
Intermediate.	☐ -2	☐ -2
Advanced.	☐ -3	☐ -3

7. Which of the following best describes your job title?

Officer (CEO/President/VP/owner). . . . . . . ☐ -1 (26)
Director/head. . . . . ☐ -2
Manager/supervisor. . . . . ☐ -3
Administration/staff. . . . . ☐ -4
Teacher/educator/trainer. . . . . ☐ -5
Lawyer/doctor/medical professional. . . . . . . ☐ -6
Engineer/technician. . . . . ☐ -7
Consultant. . . . . ☐ -8
Not employed/student/retired. . . . . ☐ -9
Other (Please specify): _____ ☐ -0

8. What is your age?

Under 20. . . . . ☐ -1 (27)
21-29. . . . . ☐ -2
30-39. . . . . ☐ -3
40-49. . . . . ☐ -4
50-59. . . . . ☐ -5
60 or over. . . . . ☐ -6

9. Are you:

Male. . . . . ☐ -1 (28)
Female. . . . . ☐ -2

Thank you for your assistance with this important information! Please write your address below to receive our free catalog.

Name: _____

Address: _____

City/State/Zip: _____

Fold here to mail.

3164-02-14